Four Tragic Deaths

Harold C. Allen

Pendulum Press, Inc.   West Haven, Connecticut   El Monte, California

ISBN 0-88301-143-4

Library of Congress Catalog Card Number 73-92622

Published by
Pendulum Press, Inc.
An Academic Industries, Inc. Company
The Academic Building
Saw Mill Road
West Haven, Connecticut 06516

Printed in the United States of America

CONTENTS

INTRODUCTION

This book is an effort to suggest the causes and significance of the assassinations of Presidents Abraham Lincoln and John F. Kennedy, the Reverend Martin Luther King, Jr., and Senator Robert F. Kennedy.

Like many American boys, this author early became a hero-worshiper, not of Babe Ruth or "Red" Grange but of a politician! This hero, a real man with great warmth and engaging personality, was not merely a name with an imposing list of achievements. Most important men about whom I have read in history books were so distant and cold that they had no realness to me. But Abraham Lincoln was a truly human sort of being about whom I could feel very deeply. His rise from humble poverty on the western frontier to the Presidency during one of our nation's critical years always aroused my respect and admiration. When I was a ten-year-old standing near the huge Lincoln Memorial, I was much aware of my attachment to "Honest Abe." Many years later on a quiet summer evening my wife and I stood with our two teen-age daughters near the roped-off steps leading to this classical monument. Quite to my surprise I experienced much the sort of emotion that had seized me as a child. But for no other political figure do I hold any personal attachment such as I have for Lincoln. It seems to me that the basic reason for my close empathy with the Great Emancipator lies in his direct relationship with me. I was with young Abe when he was working on his slate by candlelight, trying to educate himself as few frontiersmen did. His love for reading—"my best friend is the person who has just brought me a book I haven't read"—and his appreciation of books were attitudes I shared. His marvelous gift for telling stories entertained me as his physical strength and his personal courage excited me. How I admired Abe for daring to wrestle with the bully, Jack Armstrong, and in victory acquiring not an enemy but a friend. How I respected him for his skillful and successful defense of this same Jack Armstrong some years later in a murder trial. How kindly I felt toward this man as the loving father of Robert, Eddie, Willie, and Tad. Perhaps most of all, how deeply I have appreciated the grandfather image of the Lincoln I have always loved.

From 1945 to 1960 there was a lack of charisma in our national leaders, but the victory of John F. Kennedy in 1960 brought a new sense of excitement and involvement to many Americans. I had been raised in the bias against Joseph P. Kennedy with his indecent amount of wealth and his improper desire for public power. Yet, by the time Jack Kennedy had won the Presidency, he had me in the palm of his hand. His inaugural address, brief but brilliant, was embellished by the participation of my favorite American poet, Robert Frost. It was great, I thought, that this bright young man with a charming wife and delightful children had an intellectual radiance that the White House had seldom known. It was gratifying that poets and musicians, scholars and philosophers were gaining recognition by the highest officer in our country. It seemed that Europeans, Africans, Latin Americans, and other peoples of the world were discovering Jack Kennedy as a symbol of hope rather than as "the ugly American." His warmth, his friendliness, and his kindliness generated an enthusiastic response. "Ich bin ein Berliner" aroused people other than West Berliners.

President Lincoln and President Kennedy, Senator Robert Kennedy and the Reverend King all became among the best-known Americans on this planet. Lincoln was always a man of the people and the other three came to complete commitment to the whole people. All four ultimately dedicated themselves to the proposition that all men are entitled to the basic dedicated rights without regard to race, color, or creed. These men were certainly very conscious of the bitterness and hatred of bigots, most of whom might be incapable personally of perpetrating crimes of violence. All faced the possibility of violent death at the hands of assassins with a fatalistic and quiet courage.

Why did our nation lose the one man best qualified to lead wisely and generously after the Civil War? Why were we deprived of the inspired leadership of a young President in the turbulent sixties? Why was the greatest spokesman for the American Negro silenced by murder? Why was Senator Kennedy killed at just the time when his Presidential candidacy had achieved its greatest victory? The theme of this book is that the answer lies largely in the temper of the times. When honest dissent and disagreement degenerate into vicious verbal abuse, it tends to ignite the passion of a sick mind. It is in this sense that our society as a whole must share the guilt of those heinous acts of violence. The day we may call ourselves a civilized people, when we have become mature enough to discipline our tongues and pens, is when honesty and temperateness will go hand in hand.

—Harold C. Allen

PART 1

ABRAHAM LINCOLN

CHAPTER 1

FRONTIERSMAN

"As a nation, we began by declaring that 'all men are created equal.' We now practically read it 'all men are created equal, except negroes'. When the Know-Nothings get control it will read 'all men are created equal, except negroes, and foreigners and catholics'. When it comes to this I should prefer emigrating to some country where they make no pretense of having liberty." This serious criticism of the American people was voiced by Abraham Lincoln in 1855, and the words reach close to the center of his thinking. There is, of course, the other side of Lincoln—the man with a deep enjoyment of humor. He delighted in telling stories, even in what usually would be considered serious situations. On one occasion as a lawyer in court he told his story of a man charged with killing a neighbor's vicious dog with a pitch fork. The defendant was asked, "Why didn't you hit the dog with the other end of the fork?" "Why didn't he come at me with his other end?" was the answer. The light as well as the serious side of Lincoln had a purpose. Both characteristics contribute to that humane quality that has made him a man of the world and a hero of all peoples.

In 1959, at a gathering in tribute to Lincoln on the one hundred and fiftieth anniversary of his birth, the principal speaker was Willy Brandt, the West German Chancellor. In the audience of some 2,500 people there were nine ambassadors along with representatives from twenty-one countries. These foreigners had come to Springfield, Illinois, in order to express their respect and their love for a man who belongs to all the people of the world. Lincoln is viewed in Russia today as one of the greatest and best men of all times. Russians still read his speeches as well as biographies about him. Far away in Pakistan there are those who have a love for Lincoln. This affection for Lincoln often begins when the children learn to read and become acquainted with the Great Emancipator. Lincoln's ideas, his concern for humanity, and his belief in the goodness of people make him a hero for Pakistani as readily as they do for Americans, who have generally held Lincoln to be the best-loved President this nation ever had. His humble origin and his humility when he was a great and powerful man of the world bring him close to all people.

Thomas Lincoln was a very ordinary frontiersman with some limited skills in carpentry, surveying, and road-building. Even as a child he experienced much of the pain of being a pioneer when, as an eight-year-old, he saw Indians kill his father. He never was able to go to any school, and according to the autobiography of his son, Abraham, Tom Lincoln could only "bunglingly sign his own name." In 1806 when Tom was twenty-eight years old he married Nancy Hanks. Their first child was a girl, Sarah, and on February 12, 1809, Abraham was born. The home of the Lincoln family was in Hardin, Kentucky, a very poor place in which to raise a poor white family, partly because of the difficulty of having to compete with the labor of slaves. Tom Lincoln suffered the heart-breaking experiences of losing in law courts title to lands he had cleared and farmed. So, he decided to quit Kentucky for a new location where there certainly would be no problem of getting clear ownership of a piece of good land. He took his family to Indiana in 1816, a new free state that had been part of the old Northwest Territory where slavery was prohibited. Their first home on this quarter-section of 160 acres was a crude half-face hunter's camp, about 14 feet wide and of similar depth. Little more than a lean-to, it was large enough for the few household goods which had been brought from Kentucky on the backs of only two pack horses. The hut was anything but comfortable during the winter months because its heat was provided only by an open fire that was kept alive at the front of the camp. This did provide some heat, but at times it nearly suffocated the Lincolns with its dense smoke. It was a life that was full of dangers to the frontiersmen.

Among the hazards facing the pioneers, one of the worst was that of fevers. Milk fever had killed off most of Tom's cattle back in Kentucky, and in Indiana he found the same disease was common. The Lincolns lost their nearest neighbors and closest friends to milk fever, and after only two years in Indiana they suffered their first personal tragedy, the death by fever of Nancy Hanks Lincoln. Young Abe was only nine years old when his mother died, but he already felt deeply the effect of his mother's character. In his later life he would always look back upon his gentle mother as intellectual by nature, blessed with a good memory, and heroic in her ability to endure the extreme hardships of frontier life. The death of his mother was the harshest experience of his early years. Abe had his close brushes with death according to his mother's cousin Dennis Hanks who said that for Abe, frontier life was "a mighty interestin' life for a boy. But thar was good many chances he wouldn't live to grow up." On one occasion during a spring flood the young Lincoln boy tumbled into a flooded creek and came close to drowning. But one real concern of this lad was that of learning—book learning, a great scarcity on the frontier.

Young Abe's education came through what he called "littles"—brief periods of enrollment in schools. Probably the total amount of formal education was not more than the equivalent of a single year of schooling. This all took place in "Blab" schools where the children muttered their readings aloud so that the teacher would know that they were doing their work. The greatest emphasis was put upon spelling through which the children might finally learn how to read. Abe could spell "incomprehensibility" before he could read "I see a car." The chief ability of the teacher usually was his capacity to discipline the children, so that instead of the "three R's" there was "lickin' an' l'arnin'." Perhaps the best that can be said of these frontier schools is that the children left the schools a little less ignorant than when they had entered. However, Abe was almost completely self-taught. He had a tremendous desire to read, and he borrowed the scarce books whenever there was an opportunity. He did read thoroughly and repeatedly the *Bible, Aesop's Fables, Pilgrim's Progress,* and the *Statutes of the State of Indiana.* He especially cherished Parson Weems' *Life of Washington,* not only because of his great admiration for the "Father of our Country" but because he had become the owner of a copy of this book. He had placed the book, borrowed from a neighbor, in a chink in the wall of the log cabin. Rain had leaked in and had damaged the book. To pay for the damaged volume young Abe agreed to work for three days in the fields of his neighbor. Throughout his life Lincoln frequently quoted passages from his favorite books, especially the *Bible.* Very few people have educated themselves more effectively than did Lincoln, and his education ended only at his death.

For a year after the death of Nancy Hanks Lincoln, her family suffered miserably. Tom was incapable of managing his household, so his children were in dirty rags, and the house became filthy. Finally, in his simple open way Tom suddenly decided to return to Kentucky to try to persuade an old friend to marry him. This was a widow, Sarah Bush Johnston, a mother of three children. Sarah and Tom were married, and they made the hard trip to Indiana with her three children. The new Mrs. Lincoln was shocked and disappointed to find that Tom's "fine" house was actually little more than a hovel. But she worked hard to convert the shack into a decent home for her double family. She accepted Sarah and Abraham with the same deep affection that she had for her own children.

Abe deeply appreciated his good fortune and always showed his love for his wonderful stepmother. Dennis Hanks had the kindest words for Sarah Lincoln: "She was a woman of great energy, of remarkable good sense . . . and knew exactly how to manage children. She took an especial liking to young Abe. But few children loved their parents as he loved his stepmother."

Abe in his early teens was pretty much a man in size, and he could work very hard. But he didn't enjoy working in carpentry with his father; he preferred to do a variety of odd jobs for his neighbors. He did work in his father's fields, but there were times when his love for words and ideas simply got the better of him. Sometimes Tom would find his son standing on a stump in the fields preaching to an admiring crowd of workers. Tom would put a hasty end to this entertainment by driving Abe and his audience back to their work in the fields. Martha, a stepsister of Abe, said "When Father and Mother would go to church, Abe would take down the *Bible,* read a verse, give out a Hymn, and we would sing. He preached and we would do the crying." She said that on one occasion her brother caught a land turtle, threw it against a tree, and crushed the shell. "Abe then preached against cruelty to animals." This strong feeling for life even of the simplest forms showed up in Abe as early as his eighth year. At this tender age he shot a wild turkey, and although living on the frontier, he couldn't drive himself ever to fire upon any game larger than the wild turkey.

The harsh life of the frontier brought a second family tragedy for young Abe when his sister, recently married, died early in 1828. Shortly after Tom and Abe buried Sarah, Abe left home for his first independent adventure. He hired out at eight dollars per month as a deck hand on a crude flatboat, floating down the Mississippi River with a load of produce for the port of New Orleans. Shortly before they reached their destination, Abe and his partner moored their clumsy craft to the river bank for the night. During the night a band of Negroes attacked the craft for plunder. Lincoln and his partner put up such a fierce resistance that they knocked some of the invaders into the river while the rest of the vandals escaped the power and fury of the young defenders. While in New Orleans, Abe had his first close view of many of slavery's worst evils, such as the auction markets for the sale of slaves. Two years later and after fourteen years of hard work and frustration in trying to exist, Abe left Indiana and helped his father to move his family into the state of Illinois. There the Lincoln men built a cabin on the Sangamon River. This proved to be the last year for Abe to live in his father's house, and a memorable year it was. That winter of 1830-1831 was one of the coldest in the history of Illinois and came to be known as "Eighteen-Hundred and Froze-to-Death!"

During the spring of 1831, when Abe Lincoln was a young adult of twenty-one, he made his second flatboat trip to New Orleans. Upon his return to Illinois, Abe settled in New Salem, a village of about twenty-five families. He worked as a mill hand and store clerk until he volunteered for service in the militia in the Black Hawk Indian War. Elected captain by his fellow volunteers, Lincoln served out his thirty-day term, and then he re-enlisted for two additional months, this time as a private. The war with the Sauk and Fox Indians ended without his seeing any violence. In later years he loved to joke about his being a military hero, although it seems likely that he really was proud of his brief career as a soldier. However, it was not in the military that he was to achieve his fame but in politics. This career had its beginning in the tiny village of New Salem directly after the Black Hawk War.

CHAPTER 2

FROM RAILSPLITTER TO POLITICIAN

Abe Lincoln began his work as a railsplitter when he was just eight years old. During the next fifteen years he had become highly skilled with his axe and wedges, clearing land for settlements and splitting logs for rail fences—both vital to life on the frontier. He became quite well-known locally both for his skill with the tools and for his extraordinary strength. As a new citizen of New Salem, Abe was eager for changes in his way of life. Seeking a political career, he became a candidate for the state legislature prior to volunteering for militia service in the Black Hawk War. Although he was enthusiastically supported by his New Salem friends, he wasn't sufficiently well-known in the rest of the voting district to gain victory. After this political setback, Lincoln considered a variety of ways of earning a living. While he was seriously contemplating the possibility of becoming a blacksmith, he was offered the minor position of postmaster of New Salem. He was also offered a second post—that of deputy surveyor. He accepted both appointments, even though he had no experience and little knowledge of surveying. He was convinced of his ability to teach himself the basics of this trade in much the same way as he had recently taught himself the basic grammatical skills in speaking and writing. When he had become aware of his poor grammar, he obtained a grammar book which he studied until he was quite skilled in grammatical expression. In similar fashion he then studied a surveyor's manual until he became quite well-informed in that trade. Then as a resident of some importance in New Salem, Abe managed to eke out a fairly decent economic existence as postmaster, deputy surveyor, and odd-jobs man.

Defeat in his political effort did not discourage Abraham Lincoln. Although his mind was still crude and uncultured, it was an intelligent mind. As postmaster he would read the weekly newspapers aloud for the benefit of his many friends who could not read. In this way, he improved his political standing in his community while he became very familiar with the major news and issues of the day. Another political asset was his great sense of humor, a quality that showed in his storytelling. He learned early of the need for self-restraint in his relationships with people. On one occasion he had allowed his superior grasp of language and his keen wit to destroy a political opponent in a debate. On the following day, full of remorse for his unkindness, Lincoln sought out his victim to beg his forgiveness. This was a lesson that stayed with Abe throughout his life. In frontier politics his skill and his fearlessness in wrestling were quite as important as his frankness and his honesty. With all of these factors in his favor it was not a surprise that when he ran again for the Illinois House of Representatives in 1834, he won a seat as a Whig. In this first experience in the state legislature Abe Lincoln introduced three bills, and two of these were enacted into laws. Fellow legislators described Lincoln as "rawboned, ungraceful, almost uncouth; having little if any of that polish so important in society life." However, "there was a magnetism and dash about the man that made him a universal favorite." Even as a very young legislator, Lincoln showed that under his rough exterior there "dwelt a mind and heart of immense powers."

Upon his return to New Salem after his first term in the Illinois legislature, Abe began to read law in preparation for a license. In two years he was awarded a license to practice law, and he was ready to move to a town where he might properly develop his talents. As a member of the state legislature Lincoln had helped organize a movement to transfer the capital from Vandalia to Springfield. It was to Springfield, now the capital of Illinois, that Lincoln moved in 1837. Here he was accepted into the law partnership of J. T. Stuart, a prominent lawyer, judge, and Whig politician. For four consecutive sessions Abe won election to the Illinois House of Representatives. Lincoln and the state of Illinois were growing up together and were prospering together. In the legislature he soon became noted for his qualities of shrewdness, persuasiveness, and persistence. He stood out as an expert in parliamentary procedure with a thorough knowledge of the techniques of legislative maneuvering. But he was more than a parliamentarian. He was a humanitarian, even at the beginning of his legislative career.

In 1937, in the Illinois House of Representatives, Abraham Lincoln stated that "slavery is founded on both injustice and bad policy." In that year there occurred the brutal murder of the newspaper publisher, Elijah Parish Lovejoy of Alton, Illinois. The pro-slave mob had killed Lovejoy for printing harsh attacks upon slaveholding. Lincoln was furious at what he termed "mobocratic spirit." No matter how great a provocation may be, Americans must not ignore law and order. The young legislator stated: "Let every American, every lover of liberty . . . swear by the blood of the Revolution never to violate . . . the laws of the country; and never to tolerate their violation by others. Let reverence for the laws . . . become the political religion of the nation." This passion for political honesty and decency came to be a decisive factor in ending his bachelor days when he was nearly thirty-three years old.

Mary Todd was an unusual young woman of twenty-three years of age. Unlike most women of her day Miss Todd was interested and active in politics, which was considered to be very much a man's world. "Pleasingly plump Molly" was just under five feet in height but she was a bold politician. Mary and another young woman had written some letters

that were published in a newspaper as letters to the editor.
Lincoln had contributed only one letter to the series when
the state official demanded to know the identity of his harsh
critics. When Lincoln assumed sole responsibility for the
written attacks, he was challenged to a duel. Fortunately the
duel was averted but very probably the gentlemanly honor of
Mr. Lincoln drew Mary Todd much closer to Abe. Just a few
months after this political excitement Lincoln married Mary
Todd on November 11, 1842, in a fashionable wedding
in Springfield.

Abraham Lincoln was considered to be a "lawyer's
lawyer." That is, he was so highly respected by his colleagues
in the legal profession that most of his cases were those that
had been referred to him by other lawyers. He labored just as
diligently on a law case as he previously worked at splitting
rails. "The leading rule for a lawyer," said Lincoln, "is
diligence. Leave nothing for tomorrow which can be done
today." His resourcefulness paid off in unusual ways. There
was a murder trial in which he conclusively proved that a
"witness" to a murder lied in his testimony that he had
observed the murder in bright moonlight. Lincoln cited an
almanac to prove that on the night of the murder there could
have been no moonlight, since there had been no moon visible
that night. Also, he was most effective in using courtroom
language that clearly made his points. He used no wordy
cliches but he did communicate very successfully through his
clarity and his fine use of rhythm in language. Furthermore,
he was just as clear and straightforward in the matter of
determining fees for his clients. Judge Davis said of Lincoln:
"He never took from a client more than he thought the service
was worth and the client could reasonably afford to pay."
One of his greatest skills was his technique in getting litigants
to agree on some kind of compromise that would eliminate
the need for a costly court trial. This consideration for his
law clients was very much like his deep concern for his
family relationships.

Robert Todd Lincoln was the first of the boys born to Mary and Abraham Lincoln. Mrs. Lincoln said that her husband "was the kindest man and most loving husband and father." Mr. Lincoln believed that children should not be whipped when they misbehaved. Parents should try to explain to the misbehaving child why his conduct was wrong. Quite poetically he declared that "love is the claim whereby to bind a child to its parents." Certainly some of the neighbors of the Lincoln family regarded the Lincoln children as badly spoiled. The children did bring Mr. and Mrs. Lincoln great joy, but they were also sources of great personal tragedy. The second son, Eddie, was a lively bundle of joy to his parents but the little fellow died just before his fourth birthday. This terrible family loss was balanced to some extent nearly a year later by the arrival of Willie, who was followed three years later by Thomas or Tad, short for Tadpole! Willie and Tad were energetic little fellows when their father was President of the United States. Even in the White House these mischievous boys were frequently involved in pranks that some official visitors found very disturbing. During a meeting of the Cabinet in the White House, Willie and Tad stirred up more than a little excitement by firing a noisy toy cannon at the frustrated Cabinet officers. Quite suddenly this happy disorder came to an end. When the first year of his residence in the White House was nearly over, President Lincoln suffered another personal tragedy. Mischievous little Willie died and left his parents overcome with the tragedy of their loss. The great man could only say, "We loved him so." The other two sons did outlive their father although Tad died at the very early age of eighteen. Only the first-born son lived a full life. Robert graduated from a New England preparatory school, attended Harvard, became a lawyer and a businessman, and served as Secretary of War as well as Minister to England. His death came in 1926 when he was eighty-three years old. In looking at Lincoln's family life, it seems that his love for his family reflected his general good will towards people. He had come to believe that all peoples belong to the Family of Man, and he was convinced that love was the chain with which to bind a family together. Even a business partnership was regarded by Lincoln as a kind of family.

In 1844, Abe Lincoln set up a new law partnership when he accepted William H. Herndon as his colleague. These men had long been good friends, despite the fact that they differed sharply in many ways. Herndon was always Billy to Abe and the older partner was always Mr. Lincoln. For twenty-one years this partnership would thrive so that Herndon was able to say, "During our long partnership we never had any personal controversy or disagreement." And this was true in spite of the fact that Billy was a very heavy drinker while Lincoln would drink no liquor. Even in politics the partners differed quite sharply. Lincoln hated slavery, but he was willing to wait for it to die out as economically unsound. Billy, however, was a radical abolitionist eager to destroy slavery immediately. In one respect they were much alike. Both men were unbelievably untidy in their office practices. Lincoln kept a large envelope on his desk with this inscription: "When you can't find it anywhere else, look in this!" It was early in this partnership with Herndon that Mr. Lincoln decided to try his skill at politics on the national level. He was determined to run for Congress.

"HONEST ABE" BECOMES A NATIONAL FIGURE

Lincoln won election to the House of Representatives in Washington in 1846. As a Congressman he was regular in attendance, and he was industrious and hardworking. Yet, representative Lincoln was a failure! Although he undoubtedly learned much from his single term in Congress, he clearly failed to represent the Illinois citizens who had voted him into office. President Tyler had persuaded Congress to pass the bill annexing the Republic of Texas in 1846. This had led to war with Mexico when the new President, Polk, claimed that Mexican invaders had attacked American soldiers on American soil. Congressman Lincoln challenged this claim and offered his "Spot Resolution," demanding proof of the exact spot where American blood had been spilled. Although many thoughtful Americans agreed that this was an unjust war for selfish gain by the United States, Illinois Whigs overwhelmingly favored the war against Mexico. Therefore, Lincoln's constituents were angry at the position their Congressman took in branding the United States as the aggressor. As a result of this experience Lincoln was not put up for re-election by the Whigs in 1848. In fact, this Whig district sent a Democrat to Congress for the first time in its history. Abe returned to the practice of law, not to return to active politics until he had determined that his unpopularity for his Congressional record had pretty much faded away. This decision came about through the emergence of the issue that many had believed to have been laid to rest in the famous Missouri Compromise in 1820.

Senator Stephen A. Douglas, the "Little Giant" of Illinois, had introduced a bill in Congress to clear up the question of the extension of slavery into the territories. This proposal of Douglas would permit the residents of a territory to decide whether or not to permit slavery within that territory. This was the doctrine of "popular sovereignty," a principle that would bring to an end the Compromise of 1820 with its provision that there would be no new slavery in territories north of the 36°30′ line, the southern boundary of Missouri. Southerners helped to push this bill through the Congress because they were convinced that popular sovereignty would enable them to acquire Kansas as a slave state even though it was north of the Missouri Compromise Line. Lincoln, who had personally deplored the existence of human slavery, was concerned with the Kansas-Nebraska Act because it would allow the spread of slavery into the territories. "I insist that if there is anything which it is the duty of the whole people never to entrust to any hands but their own, that thing is the preservation . . . of their own liberties." Mr. Lincoln furiously attacked the notion that the extension of slavery should be permitted to a mere handful of men in Congress. In his short career as a Congressman he had demonstrated his courage by offering a bill for the gradual and compensated abolition of slavery in the District of Columbia. He had introduced the bill because of his own strong convictions, and not because of the urging of abolitionists or other anti-slavery groups. Now, eight years later, he voiced his powerful objections to the extension of slavery. "I object to it," he said, "because it assumes that there can be moral right in the enslaving of one man by another. . . .Near eighty years ago we began by declaring that all men are created equal; but now . . . we have run down to the other declaration, that for some men to enslave others is a 'sacred right of self-government'. These principles," declared Lincoln, "cannot stand together."

The greatest importance of Lincoln's return to political

speech-making in the crisis over the Kansas-Nebraska Bill lay in the creation of a national reputation for Lincoln. His opposition to Douglas, the "Little Giant," exposed him to large crowds in Illinois. It was evident that Abe Lincoln was a match for Douglas in public political debate. Even though he was self-educated, Lincoln was one of the best-educated Americans of his day, and he was well-equipped to debate any political rival. This prepared him for the crucial and very famous Lincoln-Douglas Debates of 1858. These meetings occurred in the contest for the Senate seat, then held by the Democrat, Douglas. Lincoln was the Senate nominee for the new Republican Party.

"A house divided against itself cannot stand!" Lincoln declared that "this government cannot endure half slave and half free. I do not expect the Union to be dissolved; I do not expect the house to fall; I do expect it to cease to be divided." He insisted that "wrong as we may think slavery to be, we can yet afford to let it alone where it is . . . but can we . . . allow it to spread into the national territories and to overrun us here in these free states?" During the course of the seven exciting debates that drew great crowds throughout Illinois and attracted the attention of people all over the nation, Lincoln forced Douglas to take the impossible position that slavery could be protected by law in the territories, as the South demanded. Yet, slavery could exist only where it was actually protected by police power. When Douglas made this admission, he destroyed all chance of gaining Southern Democratic support in his quest for the Presidential nomination. So the great Lincoln-Douglas Debates produced basically two major results. One was that it would deprive the "Little Giant" of any chance for the Presidency. The other effect was that it took Lincoln from his position of being a politician known by a few outside his own state of Illinois to that of a national figure. Without the debates which returned Douglas to his seat in the United States Senate in victory over Lincoln, it seems practically a certainty that the new national party, the Republican party, would not have nominated Lincoln for the Presidency in 1860.

From the time of his return to politics as a Republican in 1854 Lincoln saw his nation endure a series of crises. After the creation of "Bleeding Kansas" through the popular sovereignty of Douglas' Kansas-Nebraska Act in that year, there was one critical situation after another. Over two hundred people were killed in Kansas over the issue of slavery, and much property was destroyed. A frightful episode in that tragic period was the raid of John Brown with his four sons and three other followers at Pottawatomie Creek. The fanatical anti-slave Brown, during the middle of the night in May, 1856, broke into the cabin of a pro-slavery settler named Doyle. Although Doyle was a quiet man who had taken no part in the violence over slavery, he and his two sons were brutally murdered by the Brown raiders. A similarly brutal act took place on the floor of Congress during the same week as the raid by John Brown in Kansas. Senator Charles Sumner of Massachusetts had made a brilliant but bitterly harsh speech which he called "The Crime Against Kansas." In this speech Senator Sumner viciously attacked the senators representing South Carolina. The nephew of one of these South Carolina senators was Representative Preston Brooks, who found it necessary to avenge the honor of his uncle and that of his state. Brooks beat Sumner on his head with a cane until the Senator fell unconscious to the floor where the beating continued. Sumner never fully regained his physical or mental health after the terrible beating. His Senate seat was unoccupied for over three years in condemnation of his attacker. Representative Brooks resigned from Congress, but was unanimously re-elected as evidence of his state's support of Brooks' defense of the sectional honor. These acts of physical violence further separated the North and the South, as the moderates in both sections lost more ground to the radical abolitionists in the North, and to the similarly violent pro-slavers in the South. The climate of hatred between sections of the country was growing ever more dangerous to the very existence of the Union to which Lincoln was fully committed.

The Supreme Court of the United States contributed in 1857 to the growing sectional divisiveness by the famous Dred Scott Decision. This important case determined that the Negro, Dred Scott, could not use the courts to sue for his freedom because he was born a slave, not a citizen. The final major act in this drama that was certainly solidifying public opinion in the North against the slave position of the South was the John Brown Raid at Harper's Ferry. In October of 1859, the fanatical Brown used a small force of men to capture the government arsenal at Harper's Ferry in Virginia. Brown was certain that the slaves of the South were so miserable and desperate that they were only awaiting a deliverer to lead them into freedom. On October 18th after two of Brown's sons and eight others in his eighteen-man force were killed, John Brown was captured by militia and marines commanded by Colonel Robert E. Lee. A trial for treason found Brown guilty and he was executed on December 2, 1859. Now the abolitionists had a martyr. Now the Republican party needed to find a leader who was not tainted by any show of concession to the pro-slavery Southerners. Abraham Lincoln was the new national figure who could fulfill the requirements of the new party. The Presidential election of 1860 would determine whether the Union would survive. To this Union Lincoln dedicated his very life.

CHAPTER 4

"NOW HE BELONGS TO THE AGES"

Abe Lincoln was nominated by the Republican National Convention at Chicago in May of 1860. The young party had men of greater national prominence than the six-foot four-inch former railsplitter. However, such important leaders as William H. Seward of New York and Salmon P. Chase of Ohio were less desirable as nominees because their prominence at times had created problems for them. Lincoln's oration about the "House Divided" during the course of the debates with Douglas, caused less furor among Republicans than the claim of their national leader, Seward, that there was a "higher law" than the Constitution. Besides, Lincoln and his campaign managers had worked diligently and consistently since 1858 for the nomination. Lincoln had toured at great length through the country, giving a number of important speeches. During the year of 1859, he had traveled over 4,000 miles as he gave addresses in Ohio, Iowa, Kansas, and Wisconsin. As a brilliant politician he carefully kept himself inconspicuous as an active candidate, but at the same time he kept people aware of his availability. He strongly urged Judge Davis, his friend and future Supreme Court Justice, and his other campaign aides to avoid making any deals or commitments. In this way Lincoln would have the freedom to choose the best men for the positions in the Cabinet, if he should win the nomination and the election. Unfortunately, Davis and the other Lincoln friends did make a number of promises of jobs to men in exchange for their support of Lincoln in the convention.

In the general atmosphere of bitterness and hatred it is not surprising that gentle Abraham Lincoln was harshly attacked in many Southern newspapers. Lincoln was hailed as "Ape" Lincoln, the "Gorilla." He was mocked as "King" Lincoln while some newspaper articles called him the "Baboon." His western style of dress and his western manners were ridiculed. Even his ambling gait was an object of scorn. It might have been expected that even this kindly man of extraordinary humility would have fought back at his tormentors. However, he made no major campaign speeches. His thoughts on all major issues had already been expressed forcefully in his debates with Douglas in 1858. Many thousands more had listened to Lincoln the candidate in his year of traveling and speaking throughout 1859. Early in 1860, he had presented his great speech at Cooper Union in New York City. This was probably his most important single speech. Addressing a huge audience Lincoln had started badly and was even heckled a bit at first. Gradually he warmed to the inspiration of a large audience and he eloquently made his appeal for unity of the North against the extension of slavery beyond the Southern states. His closing plea in that speech certainly helped set the stage for his nomination at Chicago later that spring: "Let us have faith that right makes might, and in that faith, let us to the end dare to do our duty as we understand it."

During the campaign all of Lincoln's rivals for the nomination now worked hard for his election. While Lincoln remained at home in Springfield, Illinois, Seward and Chase addressed crowds of Northerners, stressing the humble log cabin background of the former railsplitter. A common joke of the critics during that campaign was: "Stephen A. Douglas was a greater man than Abraham Lincoln, for while Lincoln split rails, Douglas split the Democratic party." Joke though this was, it does much to explain the victory of Lincoln over the other nominees. When the election took place on November 6, 1860, Lincoln won every free state except New

Jersey, which split its electoral vote. On the other hand, Lincoln received no votes at all from the slave states. The other three candidates received nearly a million more votes than Lincoln, so that the Republican was a minority victor. In the decisive electoral count Lincoln had 181 votes to only twelve for Douglas, even though the popular margin of Lincoln was only 1.85 million to 1.29 million for Douglas.

No man elected to the Presidency ever had such difficult months between his election in November and his inauguration the following March. Lincoln had no governmental authority to do anything to try to prevent the secession from the Union by several of the southern states. The election of Lincoln was the signal for revolt of South Carolina, followed by the other nine cotton states. The Confederacy was set up under the Presidency of Jefferson Davis and was based upon Alexander Stephens' proposition that "the Negro is not equal to the white man; that slavery is his natural and normal condition." The nation was losing its unity while President Buchanan was doing nothing to prevent the secessions from taking place while the future President was still in Illinois.

When the time arrived for President-elect Lincoln to leave his home in Springfield, it was with mixed feelings that Abe said to his old friends, "I now leave not knowing when, or whether ever, I may return." Some Springfield people claimed that his beloved stepmother, Sarah Bush Lincoln, emotionally cried out, "Abe, I'll never see you alive again. They will kill you." Lincoln and his party en route to Washington had cause for considerable worry about plots against Lincoln and those people traveling with him. Although Baltimore, Maryland, was the last city on the itinerary to Washington, the city with its strong southern sympathies had issued no official invitation to the President-elect. There was ample evidence of plots, unearthed by the Pinkerton men. So it was decided that Mr. Lincoln should pass through Baltimore at 3:30 A.M. Southern newspapers later viewed this as an act of cowardice by Lincoln. Even many Northerners were sorely disturbed as they wondered what kind of man they had as their new President. No one who knew Abraham Lincoln ever had cause to doubt his courage. At no time had he hidden from the people his thoughts about important issues. He had taken an unpopular position in his one term as a Congressman during the war with Mexico. He had also proposed the abolition of slavery in the District of Columbia. Years later when he was back in Washington but as the President, he was strongly cautioned by the newspaperman Noah Brooks, an old friend. Brooks was worried about Mr. Lincoln's habit of walking freely about Washington after dark, even though Confederate agents were known to be in the city. Mr. Lincoln's quiet comment was: "I long ago made up my mind that if anybody wants to kill me, he will." These are not the words of a coward.

President Lincoln's First Inaugural Address centered upon his hope that the South would see that he was not an abolitionist. He openly stated that "I have no purpose to interfere with the institution of slavery in the states where it exists." It was his belief that the contract between the states was binding and could not be dissolved. The keynote of his address was reconciliation within the framework of the Union. Since no state could legally secede, all resolutions and acts of secession were insurrectionary and illegal. The Federal Government would continue to hold and occupy its own property everywhere in the country, including the South. It would try to continue to collect customs duties, administer federal laws, and deliver the mails everywhere. This meant that, even against the advice of his Cabinet, the President would attempt to hold Fort Sumter in the harbor of Charleston, South Carolina.

On March 5th, the day after his inauguration as President, Mr. Lincoln learned that Major Robert Anderson had few supplies left at Fort Sumter and that he would have to surrender the fort unless he received provisions within a few weeks. On March 29th Lincoln ordered that Fort Sumter be provisioned, and by April 12th some of the seven supply vessels arrived outside Charleston Harbor. On that morning Major Anderson's old friend and former classmate at West Point, General Beauregard, began the bombardment of Fort Sumter from the Battery. After thirty-three hours of shelling the fort had to surrender. During the artillery duel there had been one fatality—a Confederate horse—and several minor wounds. But now it was clear that President Lincoln had a choice: he could accept disunion or he could fight to keep the South within the Union. With only 16,000 men in the whole Federal Army scattered throughout the country and with many of the best trained and most experienced officers declaring for their Southern states, President Lincoln had little military power with which to enforce his will upon the seceded states. He strongly disliked violence but since he held that "the Union of these States is perpetual. . .and no State. . . can lawfully get out of the Union," he had to turn to the use of force. He was convinced that the defeat of the Union would be more than a loss to the United States; it would be a serious blow to democracy in the world.

President Lincoln had to work with a Cabinet not truly of his choosing. He had hoped to appoint a Cabinet best suited to hold the nation together but his hands were tied by the promises Judge Davis and other friends had made to win the support of Seward, Cameron, Chase, and others. However, he proved to be so strong and able a leader that he controlled the Cabinet despite Seward's expectation of taking over management of the Lincoln government. Lincoln was able to maintain a generally good working relationship among his Cabinet members in spite of some bitter rivalries, such as that between Secretary of State Seward and Secretary of War Cameron. Lincoln's custom of telling humorous stories even at Cabinet meetings sometimes angered and irritated his officers. Abe Lincoln had always needed laughter for survival. He once admitted that "if it were not for this occasional vent, I should die." Probably no President loved to laugh as much as Abe, and surely no President needed laughter more than he. Laughter became a kind of safety valve for his mental health. This sense of humor also served as a health-giving medicine to some of his listeners, for Mr. Lincoln was an expert mimic. His face was capable of most comical expressions, and his sense of timing in telling jokes was superb. He could destroy a bluff with a simple short sentence. He said of a certain windbag in Congress: "He can compress the most words in the fewest ideas of any man I ever met!" He chuckled about ideas "as thin as soup made by boiling the shadow of a pigeon that had starved to death." Being a master storyteller with a rare sense of humor must have helped Lincoln keep his sanity during those terrible years when, more than any other man, he bore the impossible burden of the Civil War.

As Commander-in-Chief President Lincoln took action immediately after the Confederate attack upon Fort Sumter. On April 15, 1861, he called for an army of 75,000 volunteers. Two days later Virginia seceded, to be followed in May by North Carolina and Arkansas and in June by Tennessee. The border states of Maryland, Kentucky, and Missouri were kept in the Union largely by Lincoln's tactful treatment of the slavery problem. The President took a firm and necessary grasp of emergency power to keep the Federal Government functioning until Congress met in special session beginning July 4th. At that time Mr. Lincoln frankly told the Congress that "these measures (such as increasing the size of the Army and of the Navy) whether strictly legal or not, were ventured upon, under what appeared to be a popular demand and a public necessity . . . trusting that Congress would readily ratify them." Fortunately, Congress did agree with the President's position and did ratify his measures as legal. The Committee on the Conduct of the War, as the principal war agency of the legislature, frequently criticized the President for his "softness" toward "timid or disloyal" generals. Yet, the President and the Committee cooperated well enough to win the war finally.

After the Battle of Antietam in September, 1862, President Lincoln issued his Emancipation Proclamation, changing the war from one solely to preserve the Union into a war to destroy slavery. The proclamation, taking effect on January 1, 1863, had several purposes. By declaring free all slaves in Confederate hands, Lincoln struck an economic blow at the South. At the same time he was attacking an institution he had always hated. "As I would not be a slave," said Mr. Lincoln, "so I would not be a master." Here he was assuming the moral burden of leadership, demonstrating to the world that this was a war not only for the preservation of American unity but also for the end of an evil—slavery. After this Emancipation Proclamation, world opinion was more strongly in favor of the North.

In November, 1863, at the site of the Battle of Gettysburg of the previous July, Lincoln delivered probably the best brief speech in all history. It has been called "a national treasure and a monument of world history." Lincoln's role was to have been minor, closing the program with a few comments after the major oration of two hours by Senator Edward Everett. Although some anti-Lincoln critics called his speech "dishwatery utterances," most people saw it immediately as a work of genius. Edward Everett's admission was that "I should be glad if I could flatter myself that I came as near the central idea of the occasion in two hours as you did in two minutes."

Mr. Lincoln was pessimistic about his chance of re-election in 1864. The war had been long and terribly costly, both in lives and in property. The popular, brilliant but unsuccessful General George B. McClellan, whom he had had to fire twice, was his confident Democratic opponent. But the American people knew their President better than politicians realized. Often Lincoln had patiently allowed many common people to visit him. More than once a general or other important official had waited while the President chatted with a common soldier or with ordinary folk. When re-elected he centered his inaugural upon this noble thought: "With malice toward none; with charity for all . . . to bind up the nation's wounds . . . to achieve a just and lasting peace, among ourselves and with all nations."

General Lee had surrendered to General Grant at Appomattox Court House, and the war was over. On April 14th, the Lincolns decided to attend Ford's Theatre to see "Our American Cousin." John Wilkes Booth slipped into the President's box and fired one shot from a derringer into the back of the President's head. The madman drew a knife, slashed the arm of Mayor Rathbone, a guest of the President, then he leaped from the box, catching his boot on a framed engraving of Washington and snagging his spur on a flag. Falling to the stage, his leg broken, he shouted, *"Sic semper tyrannis,"* and dragged himself from the theatre.

President Lincoln never regained consciousness. At 7:22 on the morning of April 15th, Secretary of War Stanton saw that the great man was dead. "Now he belongs to the ages," he solemnly announced. The mass of Northerners reacted with severe shock to the death of their leader. Many Southerners shared the sense of loss and Confederate General Joseph Johnston expressed the view of many Southerners when he said, "Mr. Lincoln was the best friend that the South had." "The bitterest enemy of the South," said a Richmond minister, "could not have devised a deeper injury . . . to the people than the murder of President Lincoln." To many Northerners the death of their "Father Abraham" was a loss such as of a father or other dear relative. The crime of John Wilkes Booth was the foul murder of a great and good President whose humane policy of reconstruction of the South was the one solid hope for peace. The very forces of hate and vengeance that Lincoln had been seeking to curb were unloosed by the action of a madman. All the people of the world were to suffer a permanent loss because of one man's crime.

PART 2

JOHN FITZGERALD KENNEDY

CHAPTER 1

WAR HERO

Patrol-Torpedo Boat 109 was a little plywood ship with thirty tough but lucky missions in the waters of the Solomon Islands. She had carried out these attacks without injury to her thirteen-man crew and with no damage to herself. In the darkness of early morning on August 2, 1943, under the command of her young officer, she was now on her thirty-first mission with two engines idling and her third at low speed. It would have been dangerous to create a white wake that might be seen on this dark sea by Japanese patrol places or by enemy destroyers. Suddenly a lookout on *PT-109* spotted the *Amagiri* bearing down on collision course at thirty knots. The Japanese destroyer sliced easily through the American craft, leaving the shattered boat in separate sections in a sea of flames fed by high-octane gasoline. It was obvious that there could be no survivors, so Captain Hanami sped the *Amagiri* into the darkness. But the Japanese had miscalculated on the almost unbelieveable luck of the American crew.

The half of the patrol boat where the commanding officer and his radioman had been on duty remained floating because of its watertight compartments. Clinging to debris near the floating section were four crewmen, and in the water, were six more members of the crew. The officer dove from his place of relative safety to swim out to his badly burned engineer, who was with another crewman with severe leg injuries. Getting these men back to the floating hulk was extremely difficult because of the swirling currents and the strong wind squalls. But finally the exhausted twenty-five-year old officer had ten survivors on the piece of wreckage. This courageous officer, who had been nicknamed "Shaftie" by his crew because he was thin like the shaft of an arrow, was Lieutenant Junior Grade John Fitzgerald Kennedy.

With no food, no water, and no medical supplies the eleven survivors discussed and argued as to their course of action. The wreckage was now deep in the water and was only a mile from a Japanese-occupied island. As the commanding officer, Lieutenant Kennedy made the difficult decision for all the men to quit the derelict and to swim to a small island about three and one-half miles away, hoping that this island would have no Japanese. The heavy plank that had been on the *PT-109* as a mount for her small cannon was to be used by nine men on their long swim to the island while Kennedy was to tow the burned engineer. For nearly five hours Kennedy swam with the straps of the injured man's life jacket firmly gripped in his teeth, frequently choking on the salty water and all the while suffering from an old back injury seriously aggravated in the collision. Finally the exhausted men reached Plum Pudding Island, a bit of land less than half the size of a football field.

After a short rest, and despite the danger of sharks and barracudas, Kennedy re-entered the water to swim a few miles into Ferguson Passage in the hope of using a lantern to signal a PT boat on patrol. In the lonely water, hours passed but not a boat appeared, so Kennedy began the return swim. His legs were so tired that they had no feeling and to lighten the task of fighting the strong currents Kennedy let his heavy boots sink to the ocean bottom, knowing that his feet would get cut on coral when he returned to shallow waters. Although his strength was nearly gone in this twelve-hour ordeal and although at times he floated aimlessly in his life-jacket, he remained conscious and clung stubbornly to the heavy lantern as the one good chance to signal for rescue. He crawled up on the shore of a tiny atoll, Leorava, and collapsed into a deep sleep. In the morning, he tried to light the lantern that he had clung to throughout his long swim. To his dismay and disgust the lantern would not operate so he left it on the tiny bit of island, Leorava, for the two-mile swim back to Plum Pudding Island. Late that morning young Kennedy struggled out of the water, his feet badly cut by coral and his stomach sick from salt water and from exhaustion. His crew greeted him as one who had returned from the dead, for they had believed him to have drowned.

Late that afternoon Kennedy awoke from a deep sleep to send Ensign Ross on the same mission into Ferguson Passage. The result was the same. Ross returned on the next day to report that no boats were on patrol and that he, too, had been carried by the ocean currents to Leovara before his return to Plum Pudding. Despite the two failures, Kennedy tried to buoy up the spirits of his men. He decided to try to move his group to a source of food—the coconuts of Olasava Island. Not only would his men have some food to keep them alive but they would be only one-half mile from Ferguson Passage. The plank again supported the nine swimmers, and the weary officer again towed the suffering engineer across the nearly two-mile stretch of sea. It was a hard trip for all, but the reward was an abundance of coconuts and, apparently, no Japanese. Ironically, on that third night, no swimmer went out into the passage, and for the first time PT boats did come through there.

On the fourth day Kennedy and Ross swam the half-mile to Naru Island which faced directly upon Ferguson Passage. To their relief they found no Japanese and to their delight they discovered some wreckage that included a crate of hard candies. Investigating the island further they came upon a dugout canoe and a large can of rain water. These items had been cached away by natives for their own emergency use. Suddenly the two Americans dove headlong into the bushes! Just as abruptly two badly startled natives dove back into their dugout canoe! Both the Americans and the Melanesians were seized with the same paralyzing fear: the other two men might be Japanese! Actually the two young Melanesians were mission-educated Christians working for Australians as observers of Japanese landing operations. At any rate, the two men paddled their dugout canoe away from Naru Island as fast as they could. Oddly, this furious haste was to give them another frightening experience.

Thirsty because of their strenuous paddling, the Melanesians decided to land on Olasana Island for a drink of coconut milk. Of course, they had no way of knowing that Americans were on the island. The approach of the dugout presented the Americans under Ensign Thom with a real problem. Hiding in the bushes unseen they might wait for the natives to leave without their knowing of the Americans' presence. But that would eliminate the chance that these might be friendly natives who could get aid and rescue for the stranded Americans. Or should they shoot the natives as possible agents of the Japanese? Ensign Thom made up his mind very suddenly; he boldly stood up and calmly walked toward the beach where the natives were preparing to land. When the natives caught sight of Thom they immediately backpaddled as fast as they could. However, since no shots were fired, they finally stopped, got up their courage, and headed back for the beach. On the shore the blonde giant stood quietly, speaking to the natives in a friendly fashion in his strange language.

This marked the beginning of a series of contacts with the friendly natives, with their Australian leader, and finally with the Americans at the Rendova PT base. Lieutenant Kennedy and Ensign Ross were rescued by a crew in a PT boat which then went on to Olasana Island to pick up the rest of the crew under Ensign Thom. At just about this time the Kennedy family back in Massachusetts was being notified by telegram that the Navy had listed Jack and his crew as missing in action.

For his courageous leadership and his superb endurance Lieutenant J/G John Fitzgerald Kennedy was awarded the

Purple Heart for his battle injury and the Navy and Marine Corps Medal for heroic action. At this time, he was seriously ill with malaria, and his weight had dropped to 125 pounds. Some years later when he was President of the United States, he was asked by a youngster how he had become a war hero. In his typically modest manner, President Kennedy answered with a smile: "It was absolutely involuntary. They sank my boat."

CHAPTER 2

"DO THE BEST YOU CAN"

Two boys were pummeling each other as if they were bitter enemies. As the youngsters wrestled about the floor, risking injury to themselves and to the expensive furniture in the beautiful home, several other children looked on with concern or with enjoyment. What was this all about? It was only a family disagreement—a large-sized disagreement in a large family. The two young battlers were Joe, Jr., the oldest of the four Kennedy boys, and Jack, two years younger. Their scraps were the normal differences that occur when brothers are close to the same age and are rivals. However, in this situation, Joe was rather stocky in build and was much stronger and heavier than the second Kennedy son. Jack attempted to make up for his light weight by sheer determination and courage. The results of these fights were nearly always victories for the handsome and rugged Joe, who managed to maintain his control over the play and sports activities of the boys. Surprisingly there seemed to be no bitterness between Joe and Jack when a wrestling fight was over. At any rate, Mr. Joseph P. Kennedy saw this as a healthy rivalry that strengthened the competitive spirit of all of his nine children. As a man, Jack would admit that Joe's aggressive personality "was a problem in my boyhood." Yet the two strong rivals did come to appreciate each other's good qualities, and a deep bond of affection grew between Joe and Jack.

Mr. Kennedy was the head of a most unusual American

family. Its eleven members made it larger than most families and its wealth enabled the family to have large homes in various places, such as Hyannis Port on Cape Cod and Miami Beach in Florida. As one of America's richest self-made men, Mr. Kennedy had become a multimillionaire through quite a range of business enterprises. He was a very dedicated father, and he took great pride in his stress upon the old-fashioned virtues of love of family and loyalty to one's country. Mrs. Rose Kennedy provided firm discipline for her four sons and five daughters. She punished them when she considered it necessary, and she had the responsibility for their religious education in the home. Although they were all good practicing Roman Catholics, Bobby, the third son, was the most devout of the children, according to Mrs. Kennedy. Such was the success of the upbringing of the four boys that they came to respect, admire, and assist one another more and more as they grew up. Mr. Kennedy's influence upon his sons could be put into his advice that went something like this: "make up your mind as to your goal, then *do the best you can.*" How this formula worked in the lives of the Kennedy men is shown by the fact that Joe, Jr. became an outstanding bomber pilot in World War II. Jack was elected to Congress, first as a Representative and later as a Senator. And, of course, he finally won election to the Presidency of the United States. The other two brothers, Bobby and Ted, were both elected to the United States Senate. No family anywhere in the world would be likely to equal or surpass such a record of public service. And no family who gave so much to their country would suffer deeper grief as a result of their public service.

A valuable part of Jack's early education in Bronxville, a New York City suburb, came from being a Kennedy. He and his brothers gained a great deal of information and understanding about important current events from their father. Mr. Kennedy would often talk seriously with his children at dinner and in the family library after dinner. Much of this conversation concerned American politics and economic issues. Both Mr. Kennedy and his wife had been raised in families that had played important roles in Boston politics. Grandfather Patrick J. Kennedy had been a ward boss for the Democratic party in East Boston. The maternal grandfather was John F. Fitzgerald, the famous "Honey Fitz," who was the first Irish-American to become Mayor of Boston. Joseph Kennedy also had political ambitions, especially after helping Franklin Delano Roosevelt to win the Presidency in the election of 1932. Early in 1933, the new President appointed Mr. Kennedy to the office of chairman of the newly created federal agency, the Security Exchange Commission. Mr. Kennedy's job was to try to steer the investment part of the American economy back into healthy activity. This was to be one means of bringing the Great Depression to an end. Mr. Kennedy did not perform that miracle—he didn't end the Depression. However, he amazed his many critics with his excellent administration of the agency. After over a year of success in the SEC, he resigned from that position to become head of the United States Maritime Commission. Again his leadership ability was clearly shown and he was rewarded with the appointment as Ambassador to England. That an Irish Catholic from Boston should fill that important diplomatic post shocked a great many prejudiced Americans, who bitterly resented his political successes. The appointment did indicate beyond doubt that talent and dedication could raise a man to high positions in government. Certainly a father with such rich experience in public office could teach his sons much about national and world affairs.

Jack's formal education in the preparatory school phase began when he was thirteen years old and entered the Catholic Canterbury School in Connecticut. He found life at school quite difficult for a few months because he sorely missed the fun, games, and frolic of his tightly-knit family. However, he didn't allow homesickness to get the better of him. He threw himself into athletics and he did moderately well in his classwork. He tended only to get by with passing grades in those subject areas that had no particular interest for him. Foreign languages and science did not excite him, but he was an excellent student of English literature, and he did very well in history. In his early childhood, he had developed very good reading skills and he had always loved to read. He also had unusual powers of concentration. When he was interested in a book, he could read without being disturbed by noisy bull sessions of his friends in his room. He subscribed to *The New York Times* and to a news magazine so that he could keep up with current affairs.

As he became more mature, he tended to apply himself conscientiously to those subjects that he did not really enjoy. He finally learned to discipline himself in line with his father's advice, taking pride in working hardest in those subjects that he found less interesting than literature and history. His career at Canterbury was cut short in the spring by an attack of appendicitis that caused him to lose the spring semester. When he re-entered school in the fall after his illness, he attended another Connecticut preparatory school, Choate. In this non-sectarian school, Jack joined his brother, Joe, already an outstanding school athlete. Jack had to settle for intra-mural sports because he was still much too small and too light for the demands of interscholastic sports. The football coach at Choate later recalled Joe as a fine athlete but "Jack made up for what he lacked in athletic ability with fight." It was while they were students at Choate that the two older Kennedy boys became solid friends, each acquiring a keen appreciation of the other's good qualities. Some of their friends from this period of their lives disagree somewhat on the personalities of the brothers. Some claim that Jack was very quiet and shy while others assert that it was Joe who was harder to get to know.

After Jack's last and best year in prep school, one in which he finally worked consistently hard, he was rewarded with a trip to London. Now eighteen years old, he was a handsome young man. He was tall, lean, and hard-muscled from much rugged exercise and from the sports he loved, especially tennis, golf, and crew. During his visit to England in 1935, Jack was to study briefly with Harold J. Laski, the famous economist who had taught young Joe during the previous summer. However, Jack had an attack of jaundice and wasn't able to make the trip. He was not fully recovered when the college year began in the fall. During Jack's senior year at Choate, he had produced grades that enabled him to enter Princeton University in New Jersey. Despite the great wealth of his father, Jack had never been spoiled with easy money, and at Princeton he chose to room in an almost painfully plain dormitory. In this old college building he and his two roommates lived on the third floor while the bathroom facilities were in the basement. But life at Princeton was great—until ill health dogged Jack again. Jaundice made him so ill that he had to take a medical leave from Princeton. He spent much of that winter of 1935-1936 trying to regain good health in the brilliant sunshine of Arizona.

Physically fit to resume college work, Jack decided to switch to Harvard College in Massachusetts, the state where he was born. By this time his brother Joe was a member of the senior class in that college. Jack found Harvard very much to his liking. Although he was still too light for varsity football, he did try out vigorously for the team, only to be cut from the squad. Undiscouraged, he went out for junior varsity football where he distinguished himself by his passion to do his very best. This effort proved to be very costly because he suffered a serious back injury—the ailment badly aggravated later when his *PT-109* was destroyed by the Japanese warship. Despite illness and injury, Jack did persist in competing in swimming to such a degree that his coach said of him: "He was a fine kid, always giving it everything he had."

In his course work at Harvard, Jack tended to study rather casually until he completed his sophomore year. He

served on *The Crimson,* the college newspaper, and he be-
longed to a few social clubs like Hasty Pudding. The contacts
he made, both with fellow students and with faculty members, would later provide him with able men to serve him as
political associates and advisors. That his abilities were
noticed is indicated by the comment of one of his professors
who said, "Kennedy is surprisingly able when he gets down
to work. A commendable fellow."

It was in the summer of 1938, when Jack was twenty-
one, that he and Joe went to England to spend some vacation
time with the rest of the family. Mr. Kennedy had been
Ambassador to England since the previous year, and he
wanted his family to be united for a period. These were
frightening but exciting days in Europe, for it was appearing
more and more likely that Adolf Hitler's aggressive leadership
of Germany would bring on a major war. When Jack returned
to Harvard for the fall semester he persuaded his college
advisors to give approval to his application to study in
Europe during the spring semester. As a student of history
and government he would be able to observe history as it
was being made. He won the privilege of European study and
returned to London in March of 1939, just at the time when
Hitler was marching into Czechoslovakia. During the spring
and summer, Jack and Joe, Jr. served as ears and eyes for
their ambassador father as they traveled about much of
Europe. They spent some time in Paris and in other capitals
of Europe. They toured in parts of Poland and Russia and
went to the Mediterranean states of Turkey and Palestine.
Their reports were of such quality that they proved to be
very useful to Ambassador Kennedy. Jack came to some con-
clusions as results of his direct observations. He reported that
he was convinced that the Poles would fight rather than allow
Germany to take over the international city of Danzig. He
was right—the war did begin in September of that year with
the German invasion of Poland and the German seizure of
Danzig. Jack gained first-hand awareness of other world

problems in his travels. He saw in Jerusalem evidence of the difficult relationships of the Jews, Arabs, and British. In Germany, he was exposed to Nazi hooliganism directed against himself and his two friends, Torby Macdonald and Byron "Whizzer" White. Young Kennedy didn't leave Germany until just a week before World War II erupted on September 1, 1939. His work in Europe was done, and he returned home for his senior year at Harvard.

Jack Kennedy began his senior year as a rather important man on campus because his father was in a critical diplomatic post in the war zone. Of course, his travels and reports had made Jack known in his own right. As a very serious student now, he found his college work more interesting and more worthwhile than before his latest European venture. He worked harder than ever and took additional courses in government and in economics to give him a better understanding of European and world affairs. His work was of such quality that he was permitted to seek a degree with honors in political science. As an honors student he was required to produce a dissertation. Jack decided that his research project would be centered upon England's blundering into a war for which she was seriously unprepared. His topic was "Appeasement at Munich," and his research was so thorough that he received highest honors for his work. His message was that Britain's failure in foreign policy, made evident in the Munich Pact which sold out Czechoslovakia to Hitler, was the result of the poor condition of Britain's armed forces and of her weak, uncommitted public opinion. If the United States were to survive, it would need to re-arm as quickly as possible. This would call for citizen-sacrifice—the kind of appeal that appeared in his Presidential Inaugural Address—"Ask not what your country can do for you." The dissertation was so well received that Jack decided to re-write it for publication as a book with the title, *Why England Slept.*

Here was Jack Kennedy at twenty-three—author of a best-selling book and getting much favorable recognition for his work. But at this time, his father was getting into political hot water by his frank expression of strong isolationist views. He insisted that the war in Europe was not America's fight. He was seeing Nazi bombs falling in London, and he was convinced that England was going to be overwhelmed by the Germans. The United States should not share in that defeat, said Ambassador Kennedy. When these ideas were published in newspapers, J. P. Kennedy had to resign his post as Ambassador to England. Young Joe, like his father, also got into political troubles while he was a member of the Massachusetts delegation to the Democratic National Convention in the summer of 1940. Joe, Jr. persisted in holding out against the third term bid of President Roosevelt, even after it was clear that F.D.R. was going to get the nomination. He also angered fellow Democrats in high places by taking a strong isolationist position like that of his father, opposing military aid to England. Jack did not agree with his father and brother on the issue of isolationism. However, political problems and differences of opinion over the war in Europe didn't prevent the Kennedy family from enjoying what turned out to be their last full family get-together. Supreme Court Justice William O. Douglas, an old family friend, described the family life well when he called it "an exciting home . . . full of fun and games and plenty of fascinating talk. It was hard for them to find anything as fascinating outside. This is why they are so attached to each other, and so secure." But the happiness at Hyannis Port—the sailing, the wild touch-football games, and the exciting tennis matches—all had to give way because of war.

Joe, Jr. easily got into a Naval Air training program but for Jack there were serious obstacles to acceptance into military service. His back, badly injured in his football playing at Harvard, made him unacceptable to the military. But in the Kennedy spirit Jack persisted in a five-months training program with physical education experts to strengthen his back. Finally the Navy accepted him, gave him a commission as ensign, and assigned him to a job in Washington. It was late in 1942 that Jack was successful in getting an assignment to Patrol Torpedo Boat School for a six months period. During this training program, he was graded as close to perfect for his skill at handling PT boats. In character, he was rated as "very willing and conscientious." This is the young man, who as a lieutenant junior grade, was made skipper of his own boat. This was the *PT-109* that was to have thirty safe assignments and one disastrous mission under her heroic young commander. Jack Kennedy was about to become a war hero.

CHAPTER 3

JOHN F. KENNEDY – POLITICIAN

The ordeal resulting from *PT-109*'s destruction by the Japanese destroyer had left Jack Kennedy in very bad health. After he was shipped back to this country early in 1944, he spent some months as a patient in the Chelsea Naval Hospital. Suddenly his serious back ailment seemed unimportant. His brother Joe was dead! Joe had won his wings as a Naval pilot early in 1942 and had become a top-rated bomber pilot in the European Theatre of Operations. Although entitled to a furlough home after a tour of duty, Joe had volunteered for a second series of dangerous missions over Europe. With the second tour completed, Joe again volunteered. This time he was to fly an experimental plane that was to be remotely controlled after a pilot and co-pilot guided it into a flying position. Disaster struck just as Joe and his co-pilot were about to quit the robot bomber to parachute to safety. The robot exploded with its ten tons of explosives intended for Nazi submarine pens. This was the first tragic death to strike the Kennedy family. Just three weeks later came the report of the death of their son-in-law, the young English husband of Kathleen Kennedy. Kathleen's death came as a third tragedy four years later when a plane in which she was a passenger crashed in France.

The great war was over in 1945, Jack had been discharged from the Navy, and like millions of ex-G.I.s, he had to decide upon a career. Service to the nation was one of the aims drilled into the Kennedy children by their father. As a millionaire, since his trust fund was given to him by his father seven years earlier, the twenty-eight-year-old bachelor was free to do as little as he chose. He was in constant pain from his badly injured back but he was unwilling to do nothing while waiting for his back to mend from the operation performed on the injury. Jack went to work for the International News Service and covered the San Francisco Conference that was setting up the United Nations. He also toured Europe and visited England again. But he couldn't get satisfaction as an observer after his own very active military career. So he resigned from the reporter's job with I.N.S. Whether he did this at his father's urging in order to run for political office in place of his late brother, Joe, is not certain. At any rate, Jack was as well prepared for a political office as a man could be. He had a good understanding of government and of history. He was the successful author of a best-selling book on public affairs. He was an avid reader of history and politics, he was a war hero, and he was a handsome young man with an attractive personality. And he had money for campaign expenses. All that he appeared to need was a suitable political job opening.

Jack Kennedy was not about to enter politics at the local level. He boldly decided that he would make his political beginning at the Congressional level. Despite the fact that he had no record of political officeholding, he ran for the House of Representatives. The "professional" politicians were a bit amused that Jack had the nerve to aim immediately for a national office. This slender young man with skin yellowed by anti-malarial pills of Atabrine would certainly need more than the Kennedy name and the Kennedy money to win a seat in Congress. But John Kennedy had other advantages working for him. In spite of his apparent shyness, he had great will power as he had proved time and again in critical situations. The Eleventh Congressional District included not only Harvard University but also some very tough slum areas of greater Boston. Because he had never lived in the district as an adult except for his years at Harvard, Jack determined to make himself known by its residents. Long before any other candidate entered active campaigning, Kennedy was out working in the district, going from door to door, shaking hands with as many people as possible, and creating his own political organization. Even Joseph Kennedy was surprised at the political image his son was producing. He "never thought Jack had it in him."

Success breeds success, and as Jack's progress was noted, more support came his way. Not only were his brother Bobby and young friends of college days working for him but also people who had found Jack to be an exciting new personality on the political scene. The nine rivals for the Democratic nomination tended to laugh off the political efforts of the novice. He was, after all, just a "spoiled rich kid." When it became evident that the "kid" was gaining support, some of his rivals attempted to smear him with scandal. This kind of opposition only spurred Jack to campaign more vigorously than ever. By day he met people in grocery stores, factories, and anywhere people could be found. At night, his vote-getting carried him even into bars. As the only war veteran among the candidates, he stressed veterans' benefits in his speeches to young men. He made a point of reaching the female voters by having house parties where perhaps twenty people would gather for coffee and a personal appearance by the candidate. Jack's personal qualities made these direct contacts especially effective because he was able to present an informal, warm, and friendly appearance. Many who had been rather scornful doubters were charmed by this handsome and very sensible speaker. Jack Kennedy fully deserved the overwhelming victory that he achieved at the polls. Modestly he told news reporters later that he had won because he was the only veteran in the contest. Furthermore, had Joe, Jr. not been killed, he would have been the Congressman. "Just as I went into politics because Joe died, if anything happened to me tomorrow, my brother Bobby would run . . . and if Bobby died, Teddy would take over for him."

John Kennedy won re-election to the House of Representatives in 1948 and again in 1950. But he had no intention of trying to hold that seat indefinitely and so he decided to run for the Senate in 1952. This was a goal blocked by a huge obstacle. The Senate seat was held by Henry Cabot Lodge of the nationally famous political family. He was campaign manager for General Eisenhower in his campaign for the Presidency and this was a heavy burden for Lodge in his own campaign. However, it would be difficult for anyone to beat Lodge when he had the full support of Eisenhower. Jack was physically handicapped by this time with his very painful back making crutches necessary at times. One of his aides in the campaign said, "When he'd come to the door of a hall where Jack was going to give a speech, he'd hand the crutches to one of us at the door, throw back his shoulders, and walk down the aisle with his back as straight as a West Point Cadet's. I'll never know how he did it." Jack's family helped enthusiastically in his campaign with Bobby serving as the manager. His mother held receptions to attract women voters and his sisters, Jean, Eunice, and Patricia, all added their energies and personalities to the campaign. The result was a solid Kennedy victory even though Eisenhower had achieved a Republican landslide that must have given Senator Lodge many Massachusetts votes.

Senator John Kennedy at the age of thirty-five married the beautiful and talented socialite, Jacqueline Bouvier, in a big wedding that was a feature of the social season at Newport, Rhode Island, in September of 1953. The handsome couple moved into their large new home in Virginia within easy commuting distance of Washington. But as Jack resumed his work as a Senator, he began to have more severe pain in his injured back. Finally he decided to have another operation on his spine even though some specialists insisted that this would be dangerous, even foolhardy. But in October, 1954, surgeons fused disks together in his spine. For weeks Jack couldn't sit up or even move. On two occasions doctors called the family to the hospital because they believed that Jack was dying. Finally after much agony and no improvement or healing, the Senator underwent a third spinal operation in February, 1955. Again he was given the last rites of the Church, but this time the operation was successful. Jack would never have a strong back and there would be pain, but he'd be able to live a fairly normal life.

While recuperating from his latest brush with death, Senator Kennedy couldn't lie completely active in mind yet doing nothing. So he had Ted Sorensen collect research materials for a writing project. The Senator set about writing a book about a few Americans who demonstrated their courage in political acts for their country. His book, *Profiles in Courage,* was such an excellent piece of historical writing that it was awarded the Pulitzer Prize. For the second time, his literary skill had enabled him to produce a best-selling book.

The 1956 Presidential election was certain to bring Republican Eisenhower against Democrat Stevenson again. The big question was this: who will be the Vice-Presidential nominee with Stevenson. JFK had some hope of winning the nomination in the open convention. At times, he led in the voting in the convention, but finally victory went to Estes Kefauver, giving Kennedy the first and only defeat in his political career. This loss turned out very soon to be something of a blessing, as Bobby Kennedy predicted. It saved Jack from being defeated in a national election with Stevenson, and it left him free to plan his next campaign strategy—for the Presidency in 1960.

JFK began his campaign very early, as he always had done in past elections. He spoke often, all over the country, and on even the most sensitive issues. When addressing a Mississippi audience he declared, "I have no hesitancy in telling (you) the same thing I told my own city of Boston that I accept the Supreme Court decision as the supreme law of the land." His audience, admiring his frankness and his courage, gave him a standing ovation. Later, in a formal address to a group of Protestant ministers in Texas, he stated very simply that "nobody in my church gives me orders . . . my responsibility is to my constituents and the Constitution. . . . It is the obligation of a public servant to defend the Constitution. . . . I do not speak for my church on public matters, and the Church does not speak for me."

On his way to the Presidency in November, 1958, JFK won re-election to the Senate by such a plurality that it brought him valuable national coverage in the news reports. Now he was ready to move ahead at top speed in his campaign for the greatest elective office in the world. A kind of "Kennedy Fever" caught up many national and state leaders. Governors, senators, and Democratic party leaders were won over to the Kennedy side. The candidate entered a number of primaries, with probably the most critical being that of West Virginia where an overwhelmingly Protestant electorate chose JFK over the Protestant candidate, Hubert H. Humphrey. Now the way was open to the convention and to victory on the first ballot. Much of the work of getting the nomination for Jack was that of his dedicated brother, Bobby. Probably the most significant events during the exciting campaign were the television debates between Nixon and Kennedy and the commitment of John Kennedy and of Robert Kennedy to the cause of the American Negro. It seems almost certain that the positive image created by JFK in the debates and in coming out clearly for the disadvantaged American Negro tipped the balance just enough to make JFK the thirty-fifth President of the United States.

CHAPTER 4

JOHN FITZGERALD KENNEDY – MARTYR

"I suspect that few men in history have ever combined natural ability with such powers of mental self-discipline." This high praise of President Kennedy came from a brilliant scholar, economist, writer, and one-time ambassador to India, John Kenneth Galbraith. Many who worked closely with President Kennedy believe that he was not only a great politician but also an outstanding statesman. In the game of politics, he showed the same kind of fierce determination to win that had always been his way of engaging in any competition. Clearly, he was that rare President who was a man of action while he was also a scholar. With his belief that education never stops, he learned constantly and rapidly. He had a passionate interest in history but not to the exclusion of poetry and other literary forms. He had a great interest in various kinds of sports and always kept some attachment to men engaged in sports, both amateur and professional.

John F. Kennedy was not unusual just because he happened to be the youngest man ever elected to the Presidency. He was unique as the first man of Roman Catholic faith to win the highest office in this country. Surely he was the only President to celebrate his election victory as he did with a touch football game with his family and friends at Hyannis Port. No President was ever a greater reader, not only of books but of about ten daily newspapers and an even greater number of magazines. His inaugural address revealed to the world that Americans had been blessed with a man capable of greatness. His oration, although brief on that bitterly cold, bright twentieth day of January in 1961, was full of wisdom. President Kennedy reminded his listeners that man had gained the power to abolish all poverty. But, he said, man also had acquired the power to abolish all human life. He pledged the commitment of Americans to the human rights of all and to the support of liberty. He promised to aid the needy of the world "not because the Communists are doing it . . . but because it is right. If the free society cannot help the many who are poor, it can never save the few who are rich." A new "alliance for progress" would aid our Latin American neighbors to overcome poverty. He urged upon all nations the need for a "quest for peace." In his simple but eloquent manner he said, "Let us never negotiate out of fear. But let us never fear to negotiate." He called upon all men to join the struggle against the common enemies of man: tyranny, poverty, disease, and war. Finally, in words that are now engraved in stone in countless places, "Ask not what your country can do for you—ask what you can do for your country." And to the people of the world—"Ask not what America will do for you, but what together we can do for the freedom of man."

An important quality for a great leader is his ability to attract very capable persons to serve as his assistants. President Kennedy was able to persuade some leaders in both political parties, educators, and businessmen to join his "New Frontier." A former Connecticut Governor, Abraham Ribicoff, became Secretary of Health, Education and Welfare. Former Illinois Governor, Adlai Stevenson, accepted the post of Ambassador to the United Nations. The President of the Ford Motor Company, Robert McNamara, was appointed Secretary of Defense. And so the new cabinet went—a group of very able men dedicated to the service of the United States. They all came to Washington, D.C., with its great demands upon their energies and their time, and sometimes at great financial sacrifice. Their willingness to serve was solid evidence of their faith in John F. Kennedy and his philosophy of the New Frontier. They didn't accept their appointments casually. When Robert McNamara was offered a position in the Cabinet, he would not accept the post until he had the answer to a simple question: "Did you write *Profiles in Courage?*" Mr. McNamara was not concerned that accepting the government appointment would cost him about $3,000,000 of expected income. The head of the Ford Motor Company was disturbed by rumors of ghost writing of the supposed Kennedy book, *Profiles in Courage.* Some people suggested that some scholar had done the writing for the President. Mr. McNamara had been so moved by the noble qualities of the book that he had read aloud parts of it to his children. If JFK was really the author, McNamara would be honored to serve the President. At any rate, President Kennedy was successful in getting for his Cabinet nearly every man whom he sought. The result was certainly one of the most talented Cabinets in the history of this country.

What made John F. Kennedy outstanding during his 1,000 days in the White House? It was surely a combination of many factors, and among these was his unusual talent for learning his job. Walter Heller, a brilliant economist, declared that he had given the President a twelve-page paper on a difficult economic problem. Within one hour at a Cabinet meeting, the President "had read it and was quoting from it!" As Professor Galbraith of Harvard put it: "None of the most knowledgeable of the President's advisors was half so well-informed as the President himself." One clue to his ability to gain so much information and understanding about this country's economic, political, social, and diplomatic problems was Mr. Kennedy's creation of a relationship with his chief officials. He said, "It is a mistake to have just one person working on one subject because then you don't get any clash of ideas, and therefore have no opportunity for choice." His advisors would be spokes, all connected to the hub which would be the President. Although he was open to advice on all sides, JFK did his own thinking and made his own decisions.

During the 1,000 days of his brief administration, President Kennedy had to make decisions in a number of extremely important and complex matters. Within three months of his taking office, he had the ordeal of the Bay of Pigs. This ill-fated invasion attempt of Cuban exiles to drive Castro out of Cuba was planned by exiles with the aid of the American intelligence agency, the C.I.A., months before Kennedy became President. Even though this was a design supported by the Eisenhower Administration, the Kennedy government received the blame for the disaster since it occurred in April, 1961, when JFK was President. It is much to the credit of the young President that he refused to try to pass on the blame to his predecessors or to the C.I.A. that had set up the operation. He accepted the Bay of Pigs as his responsibility since he had not overruled it. Hardly had concern for that defeat begun to wane when American diplomacy was put to another terrible test. On August 17, 1961, the construction of the Berlin Wall was begun by the East German Communists. President Kennedy increased the token force of American soldiers in Berlin to persuade the Westerners as well as the Communists that the American position in support of a free West Berlin was firm. This was a calculated risk that JFK regarded as necessary. His opinion was that there was one chance in five that World War III would come out of the confrontation in Berlin. Fortunately, his firm stand produced a stand-off. The Wall remained, but so did West Berlin remain free of Communist control. But this Berlin Crisis did lead to Communist pressures elsewhere, as in Cuba.

In October, 1962, the world came to the brink of thermonuclear destruction. American U-2 flights over Castro's Cuba had revealed that missile launching sites had been prepared on this island, only about ninety miles from the mainland of the United States. After most serious study of the problem and after deep soul-searching, JFK determined upon the firm course of declaring a quarantine on the shipment of Russian missiles to Cuba. Russian ships were turned back, the missiles were dismantled, and the threat to the United States was removed. It had been a frightful decision to have to make—and time proved it to have been the correct one for JFK. It won for him the respect of his adversary, Khrushchev, and so led to meetings of the leaders of the world's two great powers that ultimately produced the Nuclear Test Ban Treaty. President Kennedy regarded this treaty as the greatest achievement of his Administration.

The 1,000 days of the Kennedy Presidency were not concerned solely with critical diplomatic matters where the existence of mankind was hanging by a thread. The White House became a cultural center as Mrs. Kennedy did much to convert the executive mansion into a living museum of American culture. Many millions of Americans enjoyed a televised tour conducted by the charming First Lady as she described interesting features of the various rooms in the White House. Mrs. Kennedy also encouraged the performing arts by her success in getting great artists to perform in the White House. Pablo Casals, Igor Stravinsky, and Leonard Bernstein were among the many figures of world fame accepting the President's hospitality. "Macaroni" also came to the White House—as the pet pony of Caroline, the President's young daughter. There were other interesting residents such as hamsters and dogs. But most interesting were Caroline and her young brother, "John John." On one occasion little Caroline appeared unscheduled at a press conference of the President, much to her father's surprise. Caroline was dressed in a nightgown, and she was wearing her mother's high-heeled shoes. At her second and last press conference she was asked what her father was doing. "Oh, he's upstairs with his shoes and socks off, not doing anything."

In the fall of 1963, JFK decided that he should do some "fence-mending" within the Democratic party. Some bitter criticism of his Administration persuaded him to take a trip to Texas to try to smooth out relationships within his party. "Don't let the President come down here," wrote a woman from Dallas, Texas. "I'm worried about him. I think something terrible will happen to him." This letter to Pierre Salinger, the President's press secretary, arrived on November 19, 1963. Mr. Salinger answered her letter, saying "It would be a sad day for this country if there were any city in the United States he could not visit without fear of violence." The President loved life and lived it well, but he had no fear of death. He said on several occasions that "anyone crazy enough to want to kill the President can do it. All that he must be prepared to do is give his life for the President's." He knew that Ambassador Stevenson had been assaulted and spat upon in Dallas. He knew that the picture of the President had been on handbills spread about the city with the label, "Wanted For Treason." This was a city that had in some years more murders than the total in England. Up to the first of November in 1963, there had been ninety-eight murders in Dallas. But John Kennedy had never turned from danger and made the tour that was to end at Dallas on the twenty-second of November. Assassination was the risk that he had to accept.

The crowd seemed cheerful and orderly as the President's cavalcade drove into the center of Dallas. Mrs. Connolly, wife of the Texas Governor, turned to the President and Mrs. Kennedy in the back seat of the car and commented, "You certainly can't say that the people of Dallas haven't given you a nice welcome." At that moment the sharp crack of rifle shots startled the procession! President Kennedy lay dying in his wife's arms with his head shattered by bullets. In a matter of seconds, a madman had destroyed the hopes and dreams of millions of people throughout the world—the hopes centered upon the courage, the wisdom, and the humanitarianism of John Fitzgerald Kennedy. Perhaps Pablo Casals expressed it best when he lamented that in his very long life "there has never been a tragedy that has brought so much sadness and grief to as many people as this."

PART 3

MARTIN LUTHER KING, JR.

"I HAVE A DREAM"

"When we let freedom ring, when we let it ring from every village and every hamlet, from every state and every city, we will be able to speed up that day when all of God's children, black men and white men, Jews and Gentiles, Protestants and Catholics, will be able to join hands and sing in the words of that old Negro spiritual, 'Free at last! Free at last! Thank God almighty, we are free at last'!"

As the last of those words rolled out over their heads and into their ears and hearts, many of the men and women in the huge gathering wept openly and without shame. This crowd of about one quarter of a million people, including perhaps 60,000 white persons, had just shared the deeply moving experience of an oration by Martin Luther King, Jr. Standing before the Lincoln Memorial in Washington, Dr. King had delivered what is likely to become one of the greatest speeches of this century. "I have a dream today" will certainly be heard through recordings by millions of people for many years to come, like the speech of John F. Kennedy at his inauguration as President of the United States. These were speeches heard literally around the world.

One might well ask why these words of Martin Luther King, Jr. were more important than the speeches presented by other prominent men in that famous March on Washington during the summer of 1963. The answer must be, in part at least, that the Reverend King was most suitable to be the spokesman against racism. Negro and white alike, American and non-American, sympathizer and critic—all had come generally to agree that at that moment, Dr. King, although still a young man, was the most eloquent representative for the American Negro. In this great speech, the leader of non-violence called for the freedom of the Negro, still held by the chains of segregation and discrimination. He said that the Negro lives on a lonely island of poverty in the midst of a vast ocean of material wealth. He is a kind of exile in his own land. The Negro today is seeking to "cash a check," the promissory note of the United States Constitution.

"America has given the Negro people a bad check," he said, "a check which has come back marked insufficient funds." This obligation must be honored and "those who hope that the Negro needed to blow off steam and will now be content will have a rude awakening if the nation returns to business as usual." "We shall march ahead with our white brothers when possible and without them when necessary. We can never be satisfied as long as a Negro in Mississippi cannot vote, and a Negro in New York believes he has nothing for which to vote." "This situation can and will be changed." Then Dr. King declared "I have a dream today."

He continued, "I have a dream that my four children will some day live in a nation where they will not be judged by the color of their skin but by the content of their character. I have a dream that one day the state of Alabama . . . will be transformed into a situation where little black boys and black girls will be able to join hands with little white boys and white girls and walk together as brothers and sisters. . . .I have a dream. . .that with this faith we will be able to hew out of the mountain of despair a stone of hope.

"With this faith we will be able to transform the jangling discords of our nation into a beautiful symphony of brotherhood. With this faith we will be able to work together, to pray together, to struggle together, to go to jail together, to stand up for freedom together, knowing that we will be free one day. This will be the day when all of God's children will be able to sing with new meaning 'My Country 'tis of thee, sweet land of liberty, of thee I sing. Land where my fathers died, land of the Pilgrim's pride, from every mountainside, let freedom ring'."

Were these grand words the noble sentiments of a truly outstanding leader of men or were they rather the empty sounds of propaganda by a person seeking to acquire greater publicity and power? It takes only a brief study of the tragically short life of Martin Luther King, Jr. to determine beyond any doubt "what manner of man" addressed the world in that stirring eloquence at the Lincoln Memorial.

BORN FREE BUT IN CHAINS

Martin Luther King, Jr. was not a child of poverty in the Negro slum of a large city. To the contrary, he first saw the light of day on January 16, 1929, in a very comfortable middle-class home in Atlanta, Georgia. This little boy had a mixed racial background of African Negro, Irish, and Indian. His father had been able to break out of the sharecropper life of the grandfather, James Albert King.

As a child the senior Martin Luther King early came to grips with the problem of racial discrimination. This occurred when the white woman for whom his mother did housework insisted that young Mike go to the back of the house to receive the sandwich through the partially closed door. The boy could see his mother in the kitchen as she ironed clothes for the white woman. Suddenly, in fury young King threw the sandwich to the ground and ran off to his home.

Somewhat later when he was twelve years old, the King boy was watching his father and the plantation-owner working over Mr. King's account as a sharecropper. The bright youngster noticed that although his father was getting credit for the cotton he had harvested, he was not getting any credit for the cotton seed, a valuable by-product of the cotton. When the boy reminded his father of this oversight, the landlord threatened to kick the boy. Soon after that incident young Martin Luther King, or Mike, as his mother preferred to call him, walked away from the plantation to try to make his living in Atlanta.

By working days while going to school at night, Mike managed to get through high school. Ambitious for higher education, he entered Morehouse College. As a college student he began his work as a Baptist minister, serving two small Atlanta churches. Before graduating from college he fell in love with Alberta Williams, whose father was quite well-to-do in the Negro business community as well as being pastor of a large Atlanta church, the now famous Ebenezer Baptist Church. The new Mrs. King was also college-educated and until her first baby was born she worked as a school teacher.

Martin was raised in a home where there was always a keen appreciation of the value of education. M. L. King, Sr. had clearly lifted himself out of the despair of sharecropping to the independence of an educated professional man. He saw to it that his children had every opportunity to develop themselves for whatever careers might attract their talents. Their home life was outstanding for its orderliness, its balance and restraint. There were family prayers to begin every day and to end every evening. It isn't surprising that in this residence of two ministers there was also the reading of Bible verses at evening meals.

In order to teach his son self-discipline and responsibility, Reverend King had young Martin deliver newspapers on a home route. But he still had time for fun, and enjoyed playing sandlot baseball and football with his friends. Even in his play as a youngster Martin's strong personality enabled him to dominate his friends. His manner of playing games was so enthusiastic that one of his boyhood chums recalls that his playing was not always distinguishable from fighting. In fact, he said, "You took a chance of getting hurt even when you were playing football or basketball for fun against him." But there was another way in which this boy could find excitement. This was the thrill of playing with words.

Reverend King and Grandfather Williams and other ministers excited little Martin with their skill at controlling the emotions of their congregations. According to the boy's mother, when this lad was only six years old, he once exclaimed, "You just wait and see. I'm going to get me some big words!" There is no doubt that all through his boyhood dreams, which included his desire to become a medical doctor, he never lost sight of his goal to move people by his ideas. His native ability to persuade others through discussion generally enabled the boy to avoid physical conflict. However, when persuasion failed, he substituted fists for words to defend his rights, although he strongly disliked fighting with sticks or knives.

Two childhood experiences came as severe jolts to the peacefulness of his little world. The first occurred when he was a six-year-old with two white children among his close playmates. When these youngsters all entered public school, the white children attended their school while Martin went to the Negro school. This didn't seem important to these children until the white mother told her youngsters that they were no longer to play with any colored children. Little Martin went home in tears and from his mother he learned for the first time what it meant to be a Negro, a descendant of slaves and a victim of a system of economic, social, and political segregation.

Two years later came the second experience that clearly showed him that he was in a minority group that must suffer. His father had taken Martin to buy shoes for the boy. A store clerk abruptly ordered Mr. King and his son to take seats near the back of the store. "No," said Mr. King, "we'll either buy shoes sitting here or we won't buy shoes at all." The comfortable life of the boy was suddenly in the past. Now he must think of himself as a Negro, not just as a person.

The neighborhood where the King family lived in a two-story home with twelve rooms was a well-to-do Negro section. Some of the largest Negro-owned business organizations in this country were located in this area. In this house Michael Luther King, Jr. was raised with his name not officially corrected to "Martin" until 1957 when, as an adult, he applied for a passport for travel abroad. There was always plenty of good food in this house, even during the Great Depression of the 1930s when about 65 percent of all Atlanta Negroes were on relief. Mr. King took great satisfaction that "we've never lived in a rented house." Their family car was generally fully paid for or nearly so.

The cross that the King family had to bear was not that of poverty but that of oppression through racial discrimination. The Reverend King was an outspoken and rather hot-tempered man who dared tell the world, "I don't care how long I have to live with this system, I am never going to accept it. I'll oppose it until the day I die." The mother of young Martin was a calm person who was slow to anger. But she urged her son not to let racial discrimination make him feel inferior to white people. "You are as good as anyone else," she said, "and don't you forget it."

Martin, or M.L. as his brother, A.D., and sister, Christine, called him, entered the public schools in 1935, but he was transferred later to the Atlanta University Laboratory School. In the Booker T. Washington High School he was a fine student, so able and hardworking that he skipped grade nine. But he was no angel; he managed to get into the minor difficulties typical of teen-age boys. Yet, according to his brother, "Martin didn't fight much. He usually was able to talk any situation to a conclusion." M.L. continued to mention his desire to become a physician, but the skills that intrigued him were still those of the orator. As a high school junior he won his greatest honor—not a varsity letter in football, not high academic grades, but first place in an Elks' oratorical contest. His subject was most appropriate—"The Negro and the American Constitution."

It was during his teens that he became more and more sensitive to the injustices that Negroes had to suffer because of their skin color. Young King had experiences that made him clearly aware of the effects of racial discrimination.

He recalled bitterly a bus trip that he took with a high school oratorical group accompanied by a Negro teacher. When these Negroes were forced to the rear of the bus by the obscene orders of the white bus driver, Martin was furious. "I don't think I have been so deeply angry in my life." These feelings were made even stronger by his experiences in 1944 when he visited Hartford, Connecticut, and some other Northern cities.

Seeing no Jim Crow signs, such as "For Whites Only," encouraged him greatly. In fact, it persuaded him that he could best fight discrimination as a lawyer, so he resolved to study law. Back home in the South after his trip he found segregation even more difficult to endure. The New England trip had been a maturing experience for this serious youngster. He worked with a new intensity and diligence so that he was permitted to skip another year of study—this time, grade twelve. So, here he was at fifteen years of age, ready for college! Quite naturally he selected Morehouse College as the Alma Mater of his father and as a college in his home town.

Morehouse College, an institution for Negro men, demanded that its serious students bring only credit to Morehouse and to themselves as Negroes. There was no toleration of senseless frivolity. M. L. King found this college to be exciting and stimulating. He was impressed by the dedication of Morehouse professors to their academic freedom. They dared to teach whatever they believed and they did this with complete honesty. For his part, King delighted some of his teachers with the seriousness and the maturity of his probing questions.

Although he was an excellent student, M.L. was not typically involved in college activities because he lived off campus with his parents. Also, he was greatly concerned with trying to determine what he must do as a Negro American. Although he was a pre-law student, he still had deep within him the dream of becoming a minister. But he was sorely disturbed by the emotionalism that he saw in much Negro religious practice. He disliked the shouting-out by members of the congregations. The "amens" and the handclapping in the services irritated his middle-class expectations of behavior.

But, the president of the college and the director of the department of religion were so stimulating in their frequent sermons that M.L. decided finally to enter the ministry. His father gave him an opportunity to prove his worthiness in the pulpit. Seventeen-year-old Martin delivered a sermon that greatly impressed not only the congregation but also the minister of this church. During the next year, 1947, Martin Luther King, Jr. was ordained as a Baptist minister and was appointed assistant pastor of the Ebenezer Baptist Church in Atlanta. Now that he was a minister, M.L. decided that he must somehow reach out to the mass of Negroes whom he was dedicated to serve.

The young Reverend King concluded that he could best acquire an understanding of his fellow Negro by working alongside him during the summer vacation months. He chose hard laboring jobs in order to get a realistic view of the plight of the unskilled Negro worker. He soon learned that there was a two-pay scale—one for the white laborer and a lower rate for the Negro on the same job. But at the same time he became convinced through his work on the integrated Intercollegiate Council of Atlanta that "we have many white persons as allies, particularly among the younger generation. I had been ready to resent the whole white race, but as I got to see more white people my resentment was softened, and a spirit of cooperation took its place."

Experience and reasoning brought him to conclude in his college newspaper that education should furnish men with noble ends rather than means to an end. He believed that most so-called educated people do not think logically and scientifically. "To save man from the morass of propaganda, in my opinion, is one of the chief aims of education. Education must enable one to sift and weigh evidence, to discern the true from the false, the real from the unreal, and the facts from the fiction. The function of education, therefore,

is to teach one to think intensively and to think critically."
Intelligence is not enough. "Intelligence plus character—that
is the goal of true education," he said. "The complete education gives one not only power of concentration but worthy
objectives upon which to concentrate." With this philosophy
of education this nineteen-year-old was ready to enter Crozer
Theological Seminary, and to compete with white students.

CHAPTER 3

FROM BOYCOTT TO NONVIOLENCE

He was always late, he was loud and boisterous in his conversations, he was laughing almost constantly without apparent cause, he was dirty, and he was unpleasant to be near. How M. L. King hated that stereotype—that unfair and incorrect image of the "typical" Negro. At Crozer Theological Seminary he went to great extremes to be early rather than prompt, silent rather than quiet, gloomy rather than serious, and neat to the point of conspicuousness. He had always been a very well-mannered and attractive person, but he felt that he had to be even more so in order to make a good impression in this small college where the Negroes were outnumbered by ninety-four to six. Later young King admitted, "I was grimly serious for a time."

That year, 1948, was terribly important to him as a Negro because it was the year of Harry S. Truman's courageous fight to win the Presidency on a strong civil rights stand. This was early in the period that came to be called the "revolution of rising expectations." This was the belief of under-privileged people in this country and in the world that the time was at hand for demanding a fair share in the material goods of the nation and of the world. Patient resignation was slowly passing out of style along with "Uncle Tomism," the practice of complete cooperation and submission by the Negro to the will of the white.

But with all his efforts to be conspicuously correct in his actions, Martin King did get into one affair at Crozer that could have been disastrous. A white student from the South charged King with turning his room into a mess in a room raid. King quietly asserted his innocence, for he had not been involved in that particular bit of horseplay. Furious, the Southerner pulled a gun and threatened King. Outwardly calm, King continued to talk quietly until other graduate students arrived to take the gun and to end the explosive situation. Before these two young men graduated from Crozer in June of 1951, they had become good friends.

The church should take a direct and active role in the struggle for social justice. This position was reached by King while he was producing a straight "A" record in his courses at Crozer. This view became a central feature of his personal philosophy as a man and as a minister. He arrived at this position through his exposure to the ideas of many great thinkers over the centuries. He read ravenously, devouring eagerly the works of many leading modern philosophers. For further stimulation for his excited mind he took extra courses at the University of Pennsylvania. He also listened carefully to famous lecturers on the philosophy of nonviolence. He was especially impressed by the thoughts of Mordecai Johnson, President of Howard University of Washington, D.C. Johnson had just returned in 1950 from a trip to India where he had talked with the world's greatest leader of nonviolence, Mohandas K. Gandhi.

Johnson was so moved by Gandhi's noble thoughts that he decided to try them out in the racial struggle in progress in the United States. Gandhi's idea was essentially that nonviolence is the use of soul force as the power of truth. Gandhi maintained that "nonresistance is the vindication of truth, not by infliction of suffering on the opponent but on one's self." He gave the illustration of nonviolence: "If by using violence I force the government to repeal the law (that I do not like), I am employing body-force. If I do not obey the law and accept the penalty for the breach, I use soul-force. It involves sacrifice of self."

President of his class and academically number one at his graduation from Crozer, M. L. King was not yet converted to Gandhi's view of nonviolence. King believed that the Indian situation was favorable to nonviolence because of the huge number of Indians compared to the tiny number of British Imperial officials. In the United States the Negro minority was only about one-tenth the number of whites, so that nonviolence could be far more dangerous to any who might dare to practice it. At any rate, King still desired to deepen his education and so he used his graduate fellowship won at Crozer to get into the Graduate School of Boston University. Here he plunged into study for a doctorate in philosophy. It was in Boston, too, that he was introduced to Coretta Scott, a native of Heiberger, Alabama.

Miss Scott had always pushed herself to be the best possible. She had been the top pupil in elementary school, and had been rewarded by admission to a missionary school which prepared her for admission into Antioch College on a scholarship. Her fine soprano voice won church jobs for her, helping her to meet college expenses. As a major in elementary school education she was to have a period of practice teaching in the public schools of Yellow Springs, Ohio, where Antioch is located. But no Negro had ever taught in the schools of that town, and Miss Scott was denied the right to practice teach.

This was a tough blow for a tough-fibred young lady who was accustomed to taking hard knocks. She admitted to having been a tomboy when she was a youngster. "I have always had a temper," she said. "Mother said I was the meanest girl. I used to fight all the time." Discrimination against her practice teaching was a thing she couldn't yet fight. She was to graduate from Antioch when King was graduating from Crozer, and like King, Coretta was to go to Boston on a fellowship for graduate study.

Coretta Scott of the New England Conservatory of Music and Martin King were introduced by a mutual friend in February of 1952. In June of the next year, Coretta decided that her love for Martin was greater than her passion for a career in music. They were married in the garden of her home in Heiberger, Alabama, with Reverend Martin Luther King, Sr. uniting his son and Coretta in holy matrimony. By the following June, the Kings were ready to move back to the South since Coretta had completed her studies at the New England Conservatory, and Martin was writing his dissertation for his Ph.D.

The decision to go back to the South was a tough one for this couple. Coretta had no desire to return to the more severe racial discrimination that she knew she would have to face again in the South. Martin had a wide choice of offers of positions in colleges and churches in the North. But he felt strongly his obligation to serve the Southern Negro, so he accepted the position of pastor of the Dexter Avenue Baptist Church in Montgomery, Alabama. He gave his first sermon as pastor in that church in May, 1954, the very month of the historic Supreme Court decision on the desegregation of public schools in America. Now, after twenty-one consecutive years of formal schooling, Martin Luther King, Jr. was prepared to become a Negro leader, a national hero, and a world figure. He had developed a forceful intellect through his diligence in a broad education. He possessed an enormous will power to attempt to achieve the great goals of his lofty ambitions. Would there be the critical combination of circumstances that would enable him to fill that role of leader of his race?

In the very year of his acceptance of the pastorate in Montgomery there was a minor incident—a woman felt like sitting on her seat in a bus. On December 1, 1954, Rosa Parks was ordered by a bus driver to give up her seat to a white passenger. Rosa politely refused to walk to the rear of the bus. "I was just tired from shopping. My feet hurt. There was no plan at all." But Rosa was a Negro and so was arrested for violating Montgomery segregation laws.

Why did this firm refusal by a mild-mannered lady

spark a movement that stirred the nation? Perhaps many Negroes believed that they could not endure insults and indignities any longer. They had suffered in the summer of that year through the kidnapping and the brutal murder of fourteen-year-old Emmet Till. This Chicago boy, visiting relations near Money, Mississippi, had been lynched, arousing to bitterness some Negroes who had previously been quiet and submissive to racial discrimination. The Rosa Parks bus incident gave the Negroes in Montgomery a cause to support, and the new minister, M. L. King, provided them with a leader for their new organization, the Montgomery Improvement Association.

December 5, 1954, was set as the date for the association's attempt to boycott the city bus system. To the great joy and much to the surprise of Reverend King, Negroes walked to work, joined car pools, and rode in wagons, but they did not use the city buses. On that morning Rosa Parks was fined ten dollars for her violation of the segregation law. Later on the same day the association decided on both policy and action.

The great problem of Dr. King was to be militant enough in his speech to his people to keep them aroused and eager for action. But at the same time he had to be moderate enough to keep the crowd under the control of its chosen leaders. "Our method will be that of persuasion," said Dr. King. "Love must be our regulating ideal. . . . We must not become bitter." Then he quoted one of the greatest of Negro Americans, Booker T. Washington: "Let no man pull you so low as to make you hate him." The organization decided to continue the boycott until the bus company agreed to some very mild demands for courtesy for all riders of the buses, for a first-served arrangement for seating, and for having Negro bus drivers on routes that were used mostly by Negroes. Their first aim was to end the vulgar practice of addressing Negroes as "Nigger," "Boy," "Black Cow," and other such degrading names. This set of reasonable demands set up the basis for a kind of crusade demanding a considerable amount of missionary zeal.

For the first time in his life the Reverend King became truly aware of the great strength in the Negro religious tradition that had for many years caused him only embarrassment. This appreciation of the Negro religious spirit and tradition grew on him until he finally felt very comfortable in its presence in the huge Negro crowds that he addressed. The Negro participation in the busy boycott delighted Dr. King. People from all over the country and even from outside the United States sent contributions to the amount of over $200,000 to keep the 300 cars operating in the pool.

However, the mayor of Montgomery joined the White Citizens' Council which declared a "get tough policy." This new policy appeared when Dr. King was arrested on a charge of speeding thirty miles per hour in a twenty-five mile zone. He was put in jail in a huge cell with bums, drunkards, and even murderers. This first jail experience shocked Dr. King. The filthy cell was, so he charged, not fit for any man, however bad he might be. But, a more frightening experience lay just ahead of him.

Coretta King had a woman visitor in her home on January 30, 1955, just four days after her husband's ordeal in the jail. When Mrs. King heard the thud of a heavy object landing on the front porch, she hurried with her friend toward the rear of the house. Suddenly a huge explosion shattered the windows in the front rooms of the house and badly damaged the porch. By her quick reaction to the sound of the bomb landing on the porch Coretta saved herself and her visitor from certain injury and possible death. Her nine-weeks-old baby was also unharmed. Within a few minutes the telephone rang, and a woman caller harshly stated, "Yes, I did it. And I'm sorry I didn't kill you all."

Dr. King hurried home about fifteen minutes after the explosion, obviously worried sick about his wife and his infant child. But when he saw a crowd of about 1,000 Negroes milling about in the street in front of his house, he nobly urged them to curb their passion. "We are not advocating violence," he said. "I want you to love our enemies. I did not start this boycott. . . . If I am stopped, this movement will not stop." With his sober counsel the crowd soon thinned out and went to their homes. Such control over his own emotions and over those of a justly infuriated crowd helped make this incident a milestone in his career. Dr. King was becoming the living symbol of nonviolence. In this crisis he gave a magnificent example of the idea in action, and he very quickly came to be recognized as a national figure. Yet, he was not truly a Gandhian at this time because he was filled with rage when he thought of the great danger his wife and child had experienced.

He was, however, clearly moving toward Gandhian nonviolence. His movement in that direction was based upon his firm belief that Negroes could never win in this country by the use of violence. Perhaps it was a white woman who really brought King to identifying himself with Gandhi's movement. A librarian, Juliette Morgan of Montgomery, had suggested that the Montgomery bus boycott had similarities with the crusade of Gandhi. This idea caught the minds of the Negro leaders, especially that of Dr. King. As a scholar trained professionally in philosophy, he thought in terms of great ideas or concepts. To use the Ganhian idea of nonviolence seemed most appropriate to the Negro movement that was already based upon Negro religious tradition. What Dr. King tried to do from this time forward was to join together the image of Gandhi and that of the Negro preacher.

CHAPTER 4

THE ROAD TO MARTYRDOM

Dr. Martin Luther King, Jr., although still a young man in his late twenties, became a national figure with the success of the Montgomery bus boycott. Within a few years other Negroes would use boycotts in other Southern cities to try to break down some of the chains of segregation laws of cities and states. However, four Negro churches were bombed, as were houses of some of the leaders, including that of the Reverend Ralph D. Abernathy.

As a famous man, Dr. King lost much of his personal privacy. There were constantly telephone calls from all over the country, but there were also obscene phone calls threatening harm to King and to his family. This invasion of his home life brought him to a crisis in his life. Should he quit his public role in order to become husband and father again, to live a normal life, or should he accept his Negro leadership as his mission in life? In the privacy of his kitchen one evening Dr. King finally decided that Negroes must be ready to lose everything, including life itself, in order to have any hope of winning freedom. "My uncertainty disappeared. I was ready for anything." Martin Luther King, Jr. had earned the right to speak for the Negro of America.

Honors and tributes were heaped upon this young leader. He was invited to address the platform committee of the Democratic National Convention in August of 1956. He was honored as a speaker in the Cathedral of St. John the Divine in New York City. He was featured in articles appearing in the most widely circulated magazines in the country. For his greatest contributions in the field of race relations he was awarded the Spingarn Medal. Colleges eagerly granted him honorary degrees but certainly among the most important honors that came to Dr. King was his election as president of the Southern Christian Leadership Conference.

This Negro organization was founded in January, 1957 by a group of about sixty leaders, mostly ministers, meeting at the Ebenezer Baptist Church. The basic aim of the SCLC was that all Negroes should "assert their human dignity. We call upon them to accept Christian love in full knowledge of its power to defy evil. We call upon them to understand that nonviolence is not a symbol of weakness or cowardice, but nonviolent resistance transforms weakness into strength." It was in his role as president of the SCLC that Dr. King was to address the largest civil rights demonstration to that time.

The focal point of the Prayer Pilgrimage of May 17, 1957, was the speech of Dr. King to the 35,000 people who had come from all over the country to this assembly in front of the Lincoln Memorial. This affair marked the third anniversary of the Supreme Court decision on school desegregation.

In his first truly national address, Dr. King criticized the two major parties for their betrayal of the cause of justice. He charged President Eisenhower with being "silent and apathetic" and the Congress with being "stagnant and hypocritical." He called for strong federal leadership in dealing with the deprivations of the American Negro. He appealed for the aid of white liberals in the drive for voter registration, which was the theme of Dr. King's speech. His philosophy came out vividly in his ringing appeal: "We must meet hate with love, physical force with soul force."

After the Prayer Pilgrimage, Dr. King was challenged by some of the other Negro leaders because of his demands for confrontation. This kind of direct action where one Negro stands up as a person for his rights disturbed those Negroes who favored the NAACP philosophy which emphasized progress through the courts and through legislatures. Dr. King had come to the belief that "pressure, even conflict, was an unfortunate but necessary element in social changes." He claimed that every individual had more than the right to break or ignore unjust laws. He had a duty to violate laws that maintained segregation. To accept any form of segregation was to accept degradation, he declared. However, he cautioned, Negroes must not foolishly use boycotts or other means of confrontation when there is no chance for success. But, fortunately, not all was work and frustration for this Negro leader.

Dr. King enjoyed a novel experience in 1957, when he and Mrs. King were guests of the Republic of Ghana, the first African colony to gain its freedom. The American visitors were excited to see at first hand a people living in a completely Negro state. From prime minister to policeman, all Ghanians were black. This visit to Ghana gave King a fresh outlook on his work and increased his hopes for eventual success. For the rest of the year he was constantly involved in making speeches. In delivering some 208 addresses during 1957 he had to travel over 750,000 miles. Yet, in all this activity he managed to complete his first book, *Stride Toward Freedom,* an account of the Montgomery bus boycott. But his involvement in civil rights took its toll on his freedom. Just as Dr. King was arrested twice during the bus boycott, he was arrested a third time in September at a hearing involving the Reverend Abernathy. At the jail he was searched and, according to Dr. King, he was "pushed and kicked" into a cell. He was first charged with loitering and later this was changed to resisting arrest. At this point he took a new and important position in his struggle for liberty: he would serve his jail sentence rather than pay a fine. However, this deeper commitment to passive resistance was opposed by the police commissioner, who personally paid the fine to get King out of the commissioner's jail. From the jail Dr. King went to his church where a protest meeting was in progress. He told his delighted followers that he would never again allow a fine to be paid on his behalf for any conviction that related to their fight for freedom.

But again he warned his people: "Blood may flow in the streets of Montgomery before we gain our freedom, but it must be our own blood that flows and not that of our white brother." He promised a happy future when "all the people of Montgomery are going to live together as brothers. There may be some delays but one day we shall all live on an integrated basis."

But not all Negro Americans were contented with the King program of nonviolence. In the Negro section of Harlem in New York City some black nationalists heckled Dr. King for his moderation. This is the same Dr. King whom other Negroes had criticized for his "radical" plea for confrontation. While he was in Harlem autographing copies of his recently published book, he was approached by a white woman who asked if he were Mr. King. Then the woman cried out, "Luther King, I have been after you for five years," as she drove a steel letter opener deep into his chest. Fortunately for the victim, no one was permitted to try to remove the weapon. At the hospital, it took three surgeons nearly three hours to get the blade from King's chest in a very dangerous operation. One of these surgeons stated that "he was just a sneeze away from death."

Ten days later, on the last day of September, 1958, Dr. King had recovered to the degree that he was able to hold a news conference. He said that he felt no ill will toward the insane woman who had made the attack upon him. However, at the same time he made a gloomy and accurate prophecy: "This experience . . . demonstrates that a climate of hatred and bitterness so separates areas of our nation that inevitably deeds of violence must erupt. Today it was I. Tomorrow it could be another leader or any man, woman, or child who will be the victim of lawlessness and brutality." This near tragedy did not turn him from his mission of nonviolence.

Early in 1959, Dr. King realized what had come to be a great dream: he traveled to India, the home of Gandhi and nonviolence. He was received with great honors, and he won Indian affection with his greeting to Nehru, the successor of Gandhi as the leader of India. "To other countries I may go as a tourist," said King, "but to India I come as a pilgrim." Nehru appeared to the King visitors as a contrast to Americans in high positions in government. Nehru, born into India's highest caste, publicly insisted upon the obligation of the fortunate Indians to share their well-being with the mass of poor Indians. Greatly impressed by Nehru's commitment to mankind, Dr. King returned to his homeland even stronger in his belief that massive government participation was necessary for success in a civil rights program. But the climate of opinion in the United States was anything but favorable to Gandhian passive resistance.

This was the year of bombings and other atrocities, such as the lynching of Mack James Parker in Poplarsville, Mississippi. There was open defiance to the federal Civil Rights Commission by White Citizens' Councils. In the North, there was a growing influence of black militants under the leadership of Elijah Muhammad, demanding that a black nation be created completely separate from white America. Negro youth movements, too, were on the rise as they twice conducted marches of protest to Washington. Such were the great demands upon Martin Luther King as the head of the nationwide passive resistance movement that he finally decided that, if he were to keep his mental and physical health he must resign his pastorate. This he did in an emotional farewell to his congregation on November 29, 1959. Now he could devote all of his time and all of his energy to his campaign of broadened aims.

"The time has come for a broad, bold advance . . . for equality . . . the psychological moment has come. . . . We must not let the present strategic opportunity pass." Not only is there to be a stepped-up campaign for voter-registration, but there must also be a full-scale assault upon discrimination and segregation in all forms. "We must train our youth and adult leaders in the techniques of social change through non-violent resistance."

The sit-down movement was about to get under way. Four Negro students sat down at a lunch counter in Greensboro, North Carolina, on February 1, 1960. Within two months, there had been sit-ins at theatres, in stores of all sorts, and even in libraries in every Southern state except Mississippi. Experts in the study of social change are generally in agreement that this new form of rebellion, the sit-in, was a direct result of the success of King's management of the Montgomery bus boycott. But youth movements tend to flare up and out rather quickly, so Dr. King determined to provide co-ordination and leadership for Negro youth.

Working with SCLC leaders, King set up a program for victory. The youth groups had to be suitably organized and they needed to set up a nationwide campaign for selective buying as an economic weapon for desegregation. There was need for volunteers willing to go to jail rather than pay fines. Most important, he said, was their need to study thoroughly the philosophy—"Resistance and nonviolence are not in themselves good." There must be the aim of reconciliation. "Our ultimate end must be the creation of the beloved community. The tactics of nonviolence without the spirit of nonviolence may become a new kind of violence."

The most obvious result of this conference was the creation of the Student Nonviolent Coordinating Committee—that is, SNNC. This organization would cause Dr. King some difficulty because SNNC was based upon nonviolent action more than upon love, which was the primary aim of the national leader. To complicate his already problem-filled existence, Dr. King was arrested by the state of Alabama for alleged income tax evasion. The ordeal of the trial resulted in more than a complete acquittal of the Negro leader. The all-white jury, by finding King innocent, made it clear that the state of Alabama had made false accusations against him.

The next test of Dr. King's character came in October, 1960, when he was arrested for violation of his probation of a suspended sentence. In September he had been given a suspended one-year sentence for driving without a Georgia license. The alleged violation of probation was his presence at a sit-down demonstration in an Atlanta store. Within one week he was in solitary confinement in prison. In the Justice Department in Washington, high officials decided that the best way to aid Dr. King would be to get a statement from President Eisenhower asking Georgia to release the man. President Eisenhower issued no statement and Vice-President Nixon had "no comment" on the fourth jailing of Dr. King. However, Senator John Kennedy did take action. He called Coretta King to express his concern about her husband. Robert Kennedy also made a telephone call—to the judge who had sentenced King to jail. Shortly after Robert Kennedy's call, the Negro leader was released on bail.

The first two years of John Kennedy's administration as President were full of disappointment for Martin King. His early optimism that this President might be different from his predecessors in giving leadership to the recognition of the equality of Negroes gave way to sad pessimism. Finally the Kennedy that Dr. King had hoped for began to emerge. After the great riot in Birmingham on May 2, 1963, which had revealed to the world the savagery of Sheriff "Bull" Connor with his high-powered water hoses bowling over little Negro children and with his policemen attacking with sticks and dogs, President Kennedy soon made his commitment clear. He was the first American President to take the official position that segregation was morally wrong. This greatly boosted the spirits of Dr. King as the President sent to Congress the strongest civil rights bill to reach that legislature to that time. Dr. King then prepared for what was to become his greatest moment—his speech, "I Have A Dream."

The horrible crime in Dallas on November 22, 1963, hurt Dr. King even more deeply than it did most Americans, shocked though most were. He saw besides the end of a great young American President the possible end of his own dream for his people. However, President Johnson continued in the spirit of Kennedy and succeeded in getting the most far-reaching civil rights laws of all time. The Voting Rights Act of 1965 was intended to give the Negro of the South voting rights after a century of denial. But one year later Negro and white liberals marching for civil rights in Chicago suburbs were hit by rocks and bottles as cars were burned and thousands of whites jeered. White backlash had become conspicuous in California and elsewhere. Negro and white civil rights workers were murdered in the South, often with no punishment for the criminals.

As Dr. King stated, for most Americans the period from 1955 to 1965 "had been a struggle to treat the Negro with a degree of decency, not of equality." White Americans insisted upon ending the brutality toward Negroes, but they had never been truly committed to helping him out of poverty or against discrimination. To Dr. King "it appeared that the white segregationist and the ordinary white citizen had more in common with one another than either had with the Negro. Most white Americans think that they want fair play and racial goodwill, but this is self-deception. White Americans are not yet willing to pay the real cost of fair treatment. Many billions of dollars must go into programs to fight poverty, ignorance, and slums," he said, "and this can be accomplished without great economic strain."

What are the choices for America? Dr. King put it very simply: "Together we must learn to live as brothers, or together we will be forced to perish as fools." There is a terrible gulf between our scientific progress and our moral progress. "When scientific progress outruns moral power, we end up with guided missiles and misguided men." Perhaps it all comes down to a simple statement by this great man: "We are inevitably our brother's keeper because we are our brother's brother." Finally came his prophetic warning: "We still have a choice together: nonviolent coexistence or violent coannihilation."

On April 3, 1968, while working in Memphis, Tennessee, for a laboring group, the Nobel Peace Prize Winner, Dr. King, told his audience that "we've got some difficult days ahead. But it really doesn't matter with me now. . . . I would like to live a long life. . . . But I'm not concerned with that now. I just want to do God's will. And He's allowed me to go up the mountain. And I've looked over and I've seen the promised land. I may not get there with you, but I want you to know tonight that we as a people will get to the promised land." On April 4, 1968, Dr. Martin Luther King, apostle for peace among races and among nations, was destroyed by an assassin's bullet.

The widow of another martyr, the late President Kennedy, lamented for the world: "When will our country learn that to live by the sword is to perish by the sword? I pray that with the price he paid—his life—he will make room in people's hearts for love, not hate."

PART 4

ROBERT FRANCIS KENNEDY

A MAN OF CONTROVERSY

"I believe that as long as there is plenty, poverty is evil. As long as the instruments of peace are available, war is madness."

"Some among us say the Negro has made great progress—which is true—and that he should be satisfied—which is neither true nor realistic."

"We must rethink all our old ideas and beliefs before they capture and destroy us. And for these answers, America must look to its young people. And we look especially to that minority of privileged men who are the students of America."

These are words of Robert Francis Kennedy, telling of his desire to end poverty, his passion for peace, his commitment to fair treatment of Negro Americans, and his belief that hope for this country lies in its youth through using their educational opportunities. Could anyone criticize such aims and ideas? R.F.K. was a man whose many supporters admired him with deep emotion, a feeling deeper than just loyalty. He was, however, the man whose critics frequently charged him with being ruthless—even brutal. What kind of man was Bobby Kennedy—a man with complete dedication to the democratic way of life, or, rather, a hard-driving politician willing to use any means to achieve his goal? Was he a heroic figure with the Kennedy qualities so obvious in Joe, Jr., hero killed in the service of his country in World War II? Did Bobby possess some of the virtues of John, killed in the service of his country as President of the United States? There can be no answer to satisfy both the admirer and the critic, but it is possible to relate many reliable facts about the man so that the reader may use evidence to form a reasonable opinion. At any rate, as is true with probably most human beings, Bobby Kennedy's character was greatly influenced by his family upbringing and by his experiences as a child.

Robert Francis Kennedy, sometimes called the "runt of the litter" because of his light weight and small physique, was born on November 20, 1925, in the wealthy Boston suburb of Brookline. Joe, Jr., Jack, and four girls had all been born in that rather plain house. Within less than a year after Bobby's birth, Mr. Kennedy decided to leave Boston for residence in a community where he and his family would be able to be generally free from the prejudice that some Bostonians had for all Irish Catholics. So, in a private railway car the multimillionaire took his family of seven children to Riverdale, near New York City. The Kennedy family lived there for nearly four years when Mr. Kennedy bought an estate in Bronxville, a town near Riverdale. It was in Bronxville where Bobby spent the important years of childhood. And what a boyhood this was!

When the stock market crash occurred in the autumn of 1929 and the Great Depression followed in a year or so, the Kennedy fortune suffered no loss since Mr. Kennedy had sold much stock before the Crash, in expectation of such a disaster. However, despite his great wealth he was careful not to spoil his children with easy money. He gave his sons rather meager allowances, which the boys generally found inadequate for their needs. As an enterprising youngster, Bobby decided to go into business for himself. He sold magazines, delivering the copies from door to door, peddling his bicycle as Porky, his pet pig, trotted along behind. However, Bobby found that carrying a load of magazines on his bicycle was hard work and a slow way to earn pocket money. So, he soon gave up the peddling for a quicker, more convenient method of delivering heavy magazines—his father's Rolls Royce driven by Dave, the family chauffeur! But moneymaking turned out to be rather dull for Bobby, much preferring the rough-and-tumble life in a family which never lacked excitement with four boys and five girls providing the action.

Joseph Kennedy was often away from his busy household, managing his many business interests in various parts of the country, including Hollywood. But he clearly dominated his home and his family by his rigorous training, especially of his sons. He worked hard to make his boys desire to excel in whatever they engaged. Games were not merely to be played for sportsmanship and enjoyment. Those were important qualities of sports, to be sure, but the Kennedy boys were also impressed with the need to win, and in the games, to improve themselves physically. Tennis for the Kennedy children was played with the same ferocity that they always displayed when playing touch football. Swimming and sailing were other activities in which there might be a winner and losers. The Kennedy boys were expected to play to win. Visitors were amazed—and sometimes dismayed—at the manner in which the Kennedy boys and even the girls played touch football on the Bronxville estate. Sometimes a Kennedy looking back for a pass while running full tilt would crash into a tree. The boys all knew the experience of coming back to consciousness after colliding with an unbending oak or maple tree. The game would resume when the injured lad got back to his feet. Young Bobby, as the least gifted by nature, needed to play even harder than his brothers and so was more accident-prone than Joe and Jack. On one occasion in a family football game Bobby dashed headlong into a barbed-wire fence. Although blood streamed from the deep cuts, he insisted on getting on with the game. This wasn't a special kind of courage—it was the Kennedy way of doing things.

In a family with nine lively youngsters it was certain that there would be some lively scrapping among the children. Although Joe, Jr. often had to fight to maintain his superiority over Jack, two years younger than he, Joe had no rivalry with young Bobby. Instead, Joe served as a teacher of the younger boy, instructing him in all of the Kennedy sports. Bobby, on the other hand, was so much older than the youngest child, Teddy, that he had no sibling rivalry with this brother. However, Bobby would often tease his sisters and sometimes they managed to get the better of him. On one occasion his sister Eunice mischievously hit him with some chocolate frosting from a cake. Taking up the challenge, little Bobby chased Eunice all over the house until it seemed that he had her cornered. He lowered his head and drove himself at his sister. Eunice side-stepped like a skillful bull-fighter and Bobby missed her, bashing his head against a table. He suffered such a nasty gash on his head that he had to be rushed off to a doctor's office for repairs. This kind of experience occurred a number of times in the growing-up days of Bobby Kennedy.

Bobby learned much about politics, as did Joe, Jr. and Jack, in the frequent after-dinner discussions that Mr. Kennedy had as a regular feature of the education of his children. Much of this kind of conversation dealt with matters very real to these boys since their father and a grandfather were very active and important in American politics as officeholders themselves. The father also saw to it that all the boys had a variety of school experiences to give them contacts with children of differing social and economic backgrounds. Bobby attended public school in Bronxville for a while and finished his elementary education in London during his father's assignment as Ambassador to England. There he learned the national games of that country, cricket and soccer. He also joined the Boy Scouts while in England, insisting quite properly on his right not to pledge his allegiance to the King. Upon returning to the United States, Bobby continued his college preparatory education in the Catholic schools of St. Paul's in New Hampshire and Portsmouth Priory in Rhode Island. He completed his prep school education at Milton Academy, a secular school near Boston. At Milton he played on the tennis team, depending mostly upon energy and drive to win rather than upon skill. As the quarterback on the school football team, Bobby was conspicuous for his extremely aggressive playing, despite his light weight for that sport. Some of his friends thought he showed his greatest courage, or nerve, by joining the school glee club, even though he lacked both a good singing voice and a fair sense of pitch.

After graduating from Milton Academy, the number three Kennedy son joined the Naval aviation program and was sent to Bates College for training for eight months. Following this period of training Bobby was transferred to the Harvard program for officer-training for the Navy. This seemed too slow a process for him, and it lacked the kind of action that Jack had seen as commander of PT-109 in Asiatic waters. Also, the tragic death of Joe, Jr. as a bomber pilot in Europe made Bobby more determined than ever to see some military action, so he quit the officer program at Harvard for a Navy enlistment. Finally, through the help of a family friend, James Forrestal, Secretary of the Navy, Bobby was assigned to active duty on the new destroyer, the U.S.S. Joseph P. Kennedy, Jr. But again Bobby was disappointed as his ship was assigned to duty in the Caribbean Sea and did not get involved in any combat. When the war ended, he was ready for more schooling, and in 1946 he entered Harvard, the college of his father and of his two older brothers.

CHAPTER 2

FROM COLLEGE TO POLITICS

Bobby Kennedy had lived in the shadows of his older brothers up to his discharge from the Navy at the end of the war. They had been more gifted physically than he and as students they had shown more ability to discipline themselves in their academic work. They had been old enough while in Europe to understand more fully than their ten-year-old brother what they saw at first hand. However, Bobby did remember vividly the shocking sight of German Nazis snapping out their party salutes to Hitler and roaring, *"Seig Heil."* He did get into military service in the war but did not see any combat, while his brothers both won high honors as war heroes. But when he entered Harvard in 1946, he possessed the maturity needed for taking part in his first political campaign. He became a vote seeker for Jack in his effort to win the Democratic nomination to Congress. Bobby modestly described his role in helping his brother: "I went from house to house ringing doorbells. I don't remember what I said to them. I guess I just asked them to vote for my brother." Whatever he accomplished, he apparently didn't hurt Jack politically because Jack won the election.

At Harvard he proved that he possessed the Kennedy qualities of courage, stubbornness, and perseverance. Although he was only five feet, ten inches and weighed 165 pounds, he persisted in competing in varsity football. According to his teammate, Ken O'Donnell, Kennedy wasn't fast or shifty but he played end "like a wild

Indian." He was a quick tough guy who worked five times as hard as anybody." In one practice session on the football field, much to the disgust of the coach, Bobby was getting blocked out of the play repeatedly by an opposing tackle. Finally the desperate end collapsed and was carried off the field. Only then was it discovered that he had been trying to play after one of his legs had been broken! However, his disappointments gave way to deep satisfaction when he finally won his varsity letter in a Harvard-Yale football game. This was the first time that he achieved a goal that both young Joe and Jack had failed to win in their athletic careers at Harvard College.

After his graduation from Harvard, Bobby served for a few months as a correspondent in the Middle East for a Boston newspaper. He was, by this time, a well-traveled young man, since he had spent two months visiting countries in South America just before he entered college. However, he was not interested in a career in journalism and travel, and he felt that he was not really equipped for a career. So he decided to prepare himself for the profession of law in the University of Virginia Law School. By this time he was a married man, but marriage presented no economic problems for this law student because he had been a millionaire since reaching his twenty-first birthday. Each young Kennedy received such a trust fund upon reaching the age of twenty-one. Besides, his bride, the former Ethel Skakel of Greenwich, Connecticut, was also a member of a family of millionaires. Among her qualities that attracted the young Mr. Kennedy was her great enthusiasm and skill in outdoor sports.

In Law School, Bobby applied himself seriously to his books in contrast to his habit at Harvard of only occasionally attending classes. But getting high grades was not the primary aim of this future lawyer. He helped to revive the Student Legal Forum, and as its president he brought some controversial speakers to the campus, among them his isolationist father, who regarded the war in Europe as an affair which this country should avoid, and the old family friend, Supreme Court Justice William O. Douglas. He also obtained Senator Joseph R. McCarthy, a man whose name was soon to be made into the household word, "McCarthyism." Most important of his achievements as Forum president was his successful fight to get Dr. Ralph Bunche to the campus. This great Negro was an important diplomat, but segregationists bitterly opposed his being invited as a speaker. This success brought RFK his first publicity in newspapers throughout the country.

RFK won his law degree in June of 1951, and soon he became the first millionaire on a $4,200 annual salary as an investigator in the Internal Security Division of the Department of Justice. This part of his career marked the emergence of what his critics have called his ruthlessness and arrogance. He explained the vigor of his legal actions as necessary in his government service to bring to justice alleged subversives or Communists as well as persons who were charged with corruption in some branch of the government. This kind of pursuit of supposed wrong-doers generally cannot be done without the creation of political enemies. And since he pursued possible criminals with the same aggressive zeal that had characterized his football playing, he aroused the anger of many people, both in the government and in the general public.

In May of the next year, Bobby left his Washington job in the Justice Department to become manager of his brother's campaign to win a seat in the Senate of the United States. He was convinced that election successes come from a combination of common sense and good hard work. His one concern was to do whatever seemed most likely to help Jack become a Senator, even if the process irritated and angered some of the old Boston leaders of the Democratic party. His basic method, which became the Kennedy system of electioneering, was to get as many people as possible involved in the campaign operations. In this major struggle against Senator Henry Cabot Lodge, also a member of a famous family in American politics, committees were set up to organize "Teachers for Kennedy," "Italians for Kennedy," "Dentists for Kennedy," and many other professional and ethnic groups. They especially worked to persuade non-voters to register and won over many new Democrats in this manner. Unlike the old politicians of the Democratic party who simply tried to win Boston by a large margin, the Kennedy brothers tried to win a substantial amount of support throughout the state. Some of these veteran politicians became angry at brash young Bobby when he suggested that they get to work filling campaign envelopes for mailing to voters. He made Governor Dever furious when he scolded the Governor for what Bobby considered a mistake that might hurt his brother's political chances. Dever was so angry that he phoned Joseph Kennedy a sharp warning: "Keep that fresh kid of yours out of my sight from now on." This split was later patched up between the Massachusetts Governor and the Kennedy campaign manager. However, John Kennedy later did say that "every politician in Massachusetts was mad at Bobby, but we had the best organization in history. You can't make an omelet without breaking the egg." And certainly no one worked harder than RFK. In one instance, a petition for the Democratic nomination requiring 2,500 signatures was presented with over 262,000 names as Bobby drove himself every day of the week, sometimes for as many as twenty hours in one day. With a Republican landslide expected for the re-election of President Eisenhower, it required a tremendous effort by the Kennedy forces to overcome Senator Lodge's great advantage. Eisenhower did win in a Republican landslide, Governor Dever did lose his fight for re-election as Governor, but Bob Kennedy did conduct a successful campaign to win a Senate seat for Jack.

When his brother entered the Senate in January of 1953, RFK began service as a lawyer on Senator Joseph R. McCarthy's Senate Committee on Investigations. He took this job at the strong urging of his father, who liked the

Republican McCarthy's public position as an anti-Communist. Jack was opposed to Bob's taking this position on the committee service because he believed that this would displease political liberals, but RFK simply said about the job: "I felt it was work that needed to be done then." Very soon, however, there was bitterness between Kennedy and Roy Cohn, who had become general counsel of the committee. Kennedy attacked Cohn for his "unfair" methods of accusation. He told McCarthy that he was wrong to let Cohn operate carelessly and ruthlessly, and then he resigned at the end of July, 1953. Certainly Kennedy was no liberal in accepting the job on McCarthy's staff, and he didn't complain much about McCarthy's behavior or of his political methods. But Kennedy made no claim at that point in his career of being a liberal. Even as a conservative politician, RFK could not accept as proper the tactics of Roy Cohn. Some years later he stated that McCarthy had promised Kennedy that he would insist upon making the committee proceedings just and fair but he failed to make these reforms because "he was loyal beyond reason to Roy Cohn."

After about six months of service on the Hoover Commission for the Reorganization of the Executive Branch, Kennedy returned to the investigating committee but not as an aide to McCarthy. This time he served McCarthy's Democratic rivals, Senators McClellan, Jackson, and Symington. The valuable assistance that he gave to this minority group of the investigating committee is evidence that Kennedy was truly opposed to McCarthy's methods of conducting inquiries. Also, Bobby obviously enjoyed open battle with Roy Cohn, as in the Army-McCarthy hearings in the early summer of 1954. On at least one occasion Kennedy and Cohn were so angry at each other that they were close to a fist fight, a scrap that RFK would have enjoyed. But he was too much a gentleman to take on the very unathletic Cohn, who went so far as to offer a challenge, "Do you want to fight now?" At this point Kennedy merely turned his back on Cohn.

It may be significant to note that some comments that Kennedy made about McCarthy were surprisingly similar to criticisms that some people made of Kennedy. RFK continued to like Senator McCarthy as a man after the Senator had lost his prestige and his power with his censure by the Senate. "I felt sorry for him," said Bob, "I liked him and yet at times he was terribly heavy-handed. He was so thoughtful and yet so unthoughtful in what he did to others. He was sensitive and yet insensitive." This loyalty to a family friend didn't end until 1957 when Bobby attended the funeral of Senator McCarthy. Perhaps the most favorable comment that can be made about RFK's experience in the Senate committee operations is that the Republicans as well as the Democrats in the Senate accepted his report on the committee hearings.

In 1956, the Democratic National Convention nominated Adlai Stevenson for President, as it had done four years earlier. The Kennedy men expected that Stevenson would offer the Vice-Presidential position to Jack. Much to their disappointment, Mr. Stevenson announced that this choice should be made by the convention. So the Kennedy group immediately launched an all-out effort to win the nomination for their man. At times it did seem that Jack would win, but the victory finally went to Estes Kefauver. This was the first political loss and a bitter defeat for the Kennedy forces, but Bobby was quick to tell Jack that "this is the luckiest thing that ever happened to you." By this he meant that with the defeat of the Democrats under Stevenson—and this result seemed most likely—Jack would have had to share in that setback had he been the Vice-Presidential nominee.

In the early fall of 1959, Bobby and Jack met with a group of their ablest advisors at the Hyannis Port home of Bobby. Here in the surroundings that he loved most, Bobby conducted much of the meeting that was to decide on seeking the Presidency for Jack in 1960. As campaign manager, again he set up the Kennedy machinery for the operations in the state primaries. When Jack, a devout Roman Catholic, won a decisive victory over Protestant Hubert H. Humphrey in West Virginia, it seemed for the first time that the old political claim was no longer true: that no Catholic could ever win the Presidency. In West Virginia, Protestants made up about 95% of the population. Kennedy's victory in that state was so impressive that Humphrey immediately withdrew from the race, leaving Estes Kefauver as Jack's chief rival. Now Bobby directed all campaign efforts toward the Democratic Convention because he believed that Jack could win on the first ballot and that he might well lose the nomination if it were to go beyond the first ballot. "We're not out here (in Los Angeles) to go to night clubs. We're out here to work," he told his staff. He made the Kennedy position on civil rights courageously clear. He directed his staff to make the position of their candidate firmly and completely in support of the civil-rights plank of the Democratic platform. Even to Southern delegations the message was to be crystal-clear, whatever this honesty might cost in Southern support for Jack. "Don't fuzz it up!" directed Bobby. The victory did come on the first ballot after Teddy had delivered a message from Bobby to the Wyoming delegation that was about to vote. The message merely stated that Wyoming could determine who would be the nominee simply by casting all fifteen of their votes for JFK. The Wyoming chairman suddenly stood up and announced that all its fifteen votes were being cast for "the next President of the United States." Thus a great victory had been won, but Bobby's greatest task still lay ahead— getting Jack elected to the Presidency over the Republican nominee, Richard M. Nixon.

CHAPTER 3

RFK IN THE SERVICE OF THE PRESIDENT

Bobby ran Jack's campaign for the Presidency with all the enthusiasm that he had always shown when working for his brother, but he proved that he was now more skillful than he had been in previous political operations. He had gained valuable experience in his service to Adlai Stevenson in the latter's unsuccessful efforts against President Eisenhower in 1956. There were small but important shortcomings that disturbed RFK about the Stevenson manner of operation. Occasionally Mr. Stevenson had kept crowds waiting for him at times when delays could easily have been avoided, as when the nominee was taking time out for coffee. Bobby felt strongly that Stevenson had not been able to reach the people or to arouse their enthusiasm because he sometimes appeared distant and aloof. Such mistakes Jack could not afford to make in his campaign of 1960 because it seemed obvious that this would be one of the closest Presidential elections in the history of the nation. When Bob found party divisions within the Democratic party, such as those existing in New York with its split between "reform" Democrats and "regular" Democrats, he shook them with his harsh statement that it didn't matter to him whether their party organizations survived the election. Angrily he told these important Democrats, "I want to elect John F. Kennedy." Certainly such head-on clashes with fellow Democrats won him more enemies than friends, but Bob Kennedy had no intention of allowing quarrels within his party to damage the chance of Jack's winning the election. It is very clear that he was playing the game of politics in the same manner in which he had always competed in sports—to win! Whether he was unnecessarily aggressive or whether he was using a suitable means of achieving a worthy goal has to be a personal decision. Surely he was using good political sense when he asked Frank Sinatra and Walter Reuther not to campaign actively for Jack. There was real danger of losing public support through the political activities of the "Rat Pack" of Sinatra and his friends, including members of the "Kennedy Clan." And Mr. Reuther, as President of the United Auto Workers and of the C.I.O., might cost Jack more votes than he might win by an active role in the campaign.

Again Bobby worked diligently to enroll new voters, convinced that this was even more important than TV advertising. He worked out plans for debates with the Republican nominee, Mr. Nixon, for televising the personalities as well as the issues to the American voters. By attending to the smallest details, including even the TV makeup for his brother's face, Bob did his best to take full advantage of this television appearance. Election experts agree that this debate won much support for Kennedy, partly because his image on TV was the more attractive one. Jack was delighted with his brother's skill in managing his fight for the Presidency. "I don't even have to think about organization," said Jack. "He's the hardest worker. He's the greatest organizer. He's fantastic!" Bobby, however, described the way in which he handled his job in rather simple fashion: "I'm not running a popularity contest. It doesn't matter if people like me or not. I don't try to antagonize people, but somebody has to be able to say no." It's impossible to determine how much credit for the Kennedy victory in 1960 should be given to Bobby's diligence, his ability, and his commitment. Only by the narrowest of margins did Jack win the election. But with the Presidency won, RFK's thoughts centered upon what this victory should mean to the country. He spoke of the young men, many of them new to politics, responsible for this achievement. "This Administration will be made up of new faces to a large extent," he promised. "We're going to bring a new spirit to government, new men who believe in a cause, who believe their jobs go on forever, not just from nine to five, who believe in the United States, not just in an Administration." Would one of these new faces in the Kennedy Administration be that of Robert Francis Kennedy?

RFK had problems! Now that he had succeeded in the effort to make his brother the thirty-fifth President of the United States he had to make some important decisions. Should he begin to work closely with his father in preparation for his taking over the management of the multimillion-dollar business enterprises of the Kennedy family? This opportunity was one he quickly turned down in favor of a commitment that his father had always encouraged in all of his sons—dedication to public service. So, should he accept appointment to the Senate seat that Jack was giving up, as a Senator from Massachusetts? Bob had another quick answer to this suggestion: "The only way I'll go to the Senate is run for it." But at that time he wasn't interested in becoming a member of the Senate. He was not willing, either, to consider seriously running for the governorship of Massachusetts in the next state election. Should he seek a job of "Assistant President" such as Sherman Adams had been in the service of President Eisenhower? No, he certainly would not be in the President's shadow, either in a special job or as a member of his cabinet. However, Joseph Kennedy strongly urged Jack to appoint his brother to the office of Attorney-General. "There's no one better than Bobby" insisted the father of the Kennedys. At first, the suggestion had no appeal to Jack, for he knew well that there would be much bitter criticism about such an appointment of his brother. Finally he decided that "he's the best man I can get for the job." So, despite the certainty of strong opposition to the appointment, Jack sought to persuade Bobby to accept the post of Attorney-

General of the United States. Bob would be the one man close to the President in whom JFK could have absolute trust. After conferences with old friends, such as J. Edgar Hoover of the F.B.I., William O. Douglas of the United States Supreme Court, and Attorney-General William Rogers, Bob Kennedy finally decided to accept the position of Attorney-General.

Attorney-General Robert F. Kennedy was a lawyer who had never practiced law. How could a man without court-room experience be a proper choice for the office of Attorney-General? Even some liberal newspapers like *The New York Times* stated editorially that RFK was totally unfitted for the job, but others were convinced that he possessed the qualities necessary for success. So, in part because of the generous support of men like the Republican Senator Keating of New York, Kennedy was approved by the Senate and entered office. The Department of Justice soon became aware of the qualities of their new boss. It was quickly evident that the new Attorney-General had outstanding leadership abilities. He quickly proved that he could recognize the abilities of others by selecting a staff that even his critics rated as excellent. One of his choices later became Supreme Court Justice Byron White, the "Whizzer" White who had been an All-American football player and a Rhodes Scholar. Two other men on his staff later were to be appointed to the post of Attorney-General. This group of brilliant and dedicated young men found that working for RFK demanded consistent and hard effort. And it seemed that hardest-working of all was the young Mr. Kennedy. He was rather careless about some matters that seemed unimportant to him. His huge Newfoundland dog couldn't read the "No Dogs Allowed" signs in the government buildings and ambled along by the side of his master. RFK did allow for some humor to lighten the drudgery of office routines, he did meet hundreds of his department's workers personally, and he made himself many friends and admirers in the Justice Department. In his quiet humor he would sometimes say, "There is tremendous advantage in having the same name as the President of the United States" as he would call the Secretary of State or some other Cabinet officer for assistance in some Justice Department matter. But when he observed something disturbing, such as a secretary reading a novel while on the job, he would take immediate and effective action, even to the point of firing a person who claimed veteran and civil service protection for her job.

No Negro was a close friend of Robert Kennedy before he became Attorney-General. His awareness of the problems that American Negroes live with was political rather than moral. That is, he had long been conscious of the value of the Negro vote, but he had little grasp of the meaning of the Negro's poverty or suffering due to various forms of prejudice. Even when he telephoned to Georgia to urge the release of the Reverend Martin Luther King, Jr. from jail during the Presidential campaign of 1960, it was very probably a political act—a vote-getting gesture. It took Kennedy some time to learn of the truths about the effects upon Negroes of generations of social, economic, and political discrimination. He had never been closely acquainted with Negroes, and his experiences before the 1960 campaign generally left him quite ignorant of life for the Negro American. Probably his actions early in his governmental career were political in purpose, like his resignation from a swanky Washington group, the Metropolitan Club, because it did not allow membership to Negroes. However, it seems that he very soon came to feel a deep concern for those Americans who were suffering from discrimination at the hands of other Americans.

In the late spring of 1961, the first year of his service as Attorney-General, he had the courage to tell an audience at the University of Georgia that he believed in the rightness of the 1954 Supreme Court decision on school desegregation. But, said he, "my belief does not matter—it is the law. Some of you may believe that the decision was wrong. That does not matter. It is the law." In that same month of May, 1961, he added action to his words by rushing 400 United States marshals to maintain public order during the violence over the "Freedom Rides." CORE had organized bus trips to show America that segregation still existed in public transportation in spite of court orders and Interstate Commerce Commission rulings forbidding such discrimination. A bus had been bombed and burned at Anniston, Alabama, and its Freedom Riders later that day in Birmingham had been attacked by white racists. A week later when a white mob in Montgomery assaulted another group of Freedom Riders, Attorney-General Kennedy sent the 400 marshals into the city. While the federal marshals were keeping the white mob from breaking into the church where the Negroes were meeting, the Governor of Alabama decided to declare martial law and to call in national guardsmen to restore order. Telephoning the Attorney-General the Governor reported that the general in charge could not guarantee the safety of the Negro leader in the church, Reverend Martin Luther King, Jr. Kennedy was furious. He snapped at the Governor, "Have the general call me. I want to hear a general of the United States Army say he can't protect Martin Luther King, Jr." This show of anger so startled the Governor that he admitted that it was he, not the general, who had expressed the fear of the job and its readiness to lynch. When the Freedom Riders set off by bus for Jackson, Mississippi, they had quite an amazing amount of federal protection. Accompanying their bus were twenty-two highway patrol cars, two battalions of national guardsmen, three Army reconnaissance planes, and two helicopters. This was sound evidence of the commitment that Bob Kennedy made to this civil rights action. These actions began to persuade many Negroes of the sincerity of the Attorney-General. This hope became a strong belief for many Negroes when RFK worked in the courts and in Congress to get for the Negroes better educational opportunities and the right to vote, basic constitutional rights of all Americans. The most spectacular of these actions centered upon a young Negro, James Meredith.

The first Negro to enter the University of Mississippi was to be James Meredith. The plan of the Attorney-General was carefully designed to save the bitter segregationist Governor Barnett from some embarrassment. The Governor would guarantee the safety of all parties concerned provided that Kennedy's marshals pulled out their guns as a show of force demanding admission for the Negro student. The Governor broke his agreement: there was violence as two people were killed and 375 were injured on the campus as state troopers stood by, watching but not interfering. Very angry but under icy self-control, Kennedy ordered 3,000 Army troops to the campus. Order was restored and James Meredith succeeded in becoming the first Negro student at "Ole Miss." Again Bobby Kennedy had proved himself to be a firm supporter of civil rights, and he came to be admired by increasing numbers of Negroes and white liberals.

During the Kennedy years in the office of Attorney-General, there were many substantial gains for freedom in the United States. He excited the admiration of liberals, and he angered conservatives by getting a pardon for Junius Scales, the only American ever to be jailed for having been at one time a member of the Communist Party. When the minister, Reverend A. J. Muste, organized a peace march upon Washington, Kennedy refused to interfere, saying that "if any eighty-year-old man wants to walk 800 miles, I don't think that endangers the country." He pleased many citizens by changing the principal work of the F.B.I. from that of fighting communism to that of warring on organized crime. Not all Americans approved of the work done by this Attorney-General, but it did appear obvious that as the number one aide to the President, Bob was very effective. Besides the responsibility for the Department of Justice he had the important duties of a member of the National Security Council. As the man closest to his brother, he was able to advise President

Kennedy in the crisis over the Berlin Wall. He helped conduct the successful negotiations that led to the test-ban treaty, considered to be the greatest single achievement of the 1,000 days of the Kennedy Administration. Bobby also persuaded the President not to attack Cuba during the missile site crisis. This, said RFK, would be "Pearl Harbor in reverse." It is perfectly clear that Robert F. Kennedy was far more than just the Attorney-General, member of the Cabinet of the President. He was the closest and most valued advisor and confidant of John Kennedy.

CHAPTER 4

FROM TRAGEDY TO TRAGEDY

"Hickory Hill," in McLean, Virginia, was a happy home for the Robert F. Kennedy family. On November 22, 1963, the master of the estate had just taken a dip in the swimming pool, and had joined his wife and two guests for a poolside lunch. Suddenly the demanding ring of the telephone interrupted the pleasant calm. The call was from J. Edgar Hoover of the F.B.I. "The President's been shot!" Bobby was shocked and for a few moments he just stood speechless. But quickly he reacted, calling the Secretary of Defense to arrange his transportation to Dallas, Texas, the scene of the shooting. Then he dashed into the mansion to dress, keeping a telephone line open for further information about his brother's condition. After twenty minutes another call was received: "He's dead!" Mrs. Kennedy began to cry softly, "Oh those poor children." Bobby's first thought was "He had the most wonderful life."

There was little time for personal grief as the older Kennedy brother took over the exhausting duties of planning the state funeral for John Fitzgerald Kennedy. Bobby sent his brother, Teddy, to Hyannis Port to give the news of their tragic loss to their father, now seriously ill with a stroke. In the heartbreaking experiences of the next few days while the whole nation was in mourning, Bobby was a man of steel, controlling the deep emotions that wanted to spill out for relief. The remarkable self-control of all members of the Kennedy family won the respect and admiration of the

American people, who witnessed the whole sorrowful affair on their television sets. RFK kept up the spirits of the Kennedy family and their close friends by his steadfast courage for some days after the crime in Dallas. But finally the strain took its toll, because the bullet that had ended the life of John Kennedy had also completely changed the life of Robert Kennedy. His sorrow showed in his face, in his manner, and in his way of life. This depression would grip his soul for some months.

Finally Bobby consented to go on diplomatic missions to the Far East for the new President, Lyndon Johnson. Upon his return after some success in his diplomacy, it was soon apparent that he and President Johnson were not firm friends. Some political advisors were convinced that Kennedy would not be Lyndon Johnson's choice for Vice-President in 1964 and some thought he'd be wise either to run for governor of the state of Massachusetts or for United States Senator from New York. His one surviving brother, Teddy, was already a senator representing Massachusetts. When Teddy suffered a broken back in a plane crash in Massachusetts, Bobby decided against running for any public office. But in June, President Johnson announced that he would not have as his Vice-President any man who was then in his Cabinet. This meant, of course, that Kennedy would not be considered for the position and he would have to decide on his own course of action. Knowing full well that he would be sharply criticized as an outsider, a "carpetbagger," he determined to accept the strong advice of friends. He became a candidate for the position of senator for the state of New York.

Victory in the Democratic state convention was easily won but the campaign against the Republican senator was difficult. Not only did he have to oppose the likeable Senator Keating whose kind words had helped win approval of his appointment years before as Attorney-General, but Kennedy also had troubles within his party. There was even an organization of "Democrats for Keating." When challenged as to his reasons for seeking a Senate seat, he answered simply, "I just want to be a good United States senator." As campaign manager for Jack he had been outstanding, but as a candidate he was rather stiff and ill at ease in his speechmaking. And he had many enemies with recollections of his services in the McCarthy and the McClellan Committees. Some union people still hated him as the Attorney-General who had fought James Hoffa until he had obtained a court conviction against that union leader. There was an image of ruthlessness that the Kennedy campaign attempted to erase. Finally Kennedy began to speak warmly in favor of Johnson, and Johnson in his turn endorsed Kennedy in his race for a Senate seat. A Johnson landslide seemed most likely to bring Kennedy to victory. Another factor in Kennedy's favor was his great attractiveness to young people, who scrambled to touch him. This youthful enthusiasm caused Bobby to comment that the voting age should be reduced—to the age of six! But even without the votes of the six-year-olds RFK won the Senate position from Senator Keating.

As a freshman senator, Kennedy was unlike the two brothers who had become members of that body before he did. Jack and Ted had patiently played the senatorial game of being seen rather than being heard. Within three weeks, however, Bobby gave his first Senate speech, and he soon made clear his impatience with the slow pace of that legislature. He had served the nation as a member of the executive branch of government, so he was accustomed to giving orders and to getting things done. He had little patience for the long hours of debate and for the great stress upon procedure that the Senate required. Yet, that he was an energetic legislator is shown by a senator's claim that RFK "is a harder worker than his brother was when he was here." In New York, he persuaded many young educators, businessmen, and lawyers to work for improvements in New York City, especially in the ghettoes of the Negro sections. Elsewhere in the country, he gained popularity as he addressed audiences in support of

Democratic candidates. It was becoming evident to many Americans that this young man would some day be our President. But his popularity faded much in 1967 when William Manchester's book, *The Death of A President,* caused Kennedy to become involved in an unpleasant public quarrel with the author. Also the break with President Johnson became greater on the issue of our role in Vietnam. But Robert Kennedy continued to hold a great appeal for young Americans. One clue to this ability may be shown in a simple incident in Washington when a young girl asked Bobby and Ted for permission to take a picture of them. "No," said Bobby, "you get in the picture, too." Then he had one of his aides take the photograph of the girl with a smiling Kennedy on each side of her.

In early 1968, an exciting political decision set off a flurry of activity. Senator Eugene McCarthy had declared himself to be a candidate for the Democratic nomination. After McCarthy had won an amazing victory in the New Hampshire primary election, Kennedy entered the race. Then President Johnson shocked most Americans by announcing his non-availability for re-nomination, and he declared his support for the Vice-President, Hubert Humphrey. Just as Kennedy achieved his most important victory by winning the state primary of California over Senator McCarthy, a vicious action of murder destroyed a second son of Joseph and Rose Kennedy. There was now a second Kennedy widow, and again there were Kennedy children without a father. The eleventh child of Ethel and Robert Kennedy would be born some months after the assassination.

Why was Robert Kennedy killed? Why was John Kennedy assassinated? Who can say? Robert had once said that "existence is so fickle, fate is so fickle." There were persons who had their reasons for hating either man or both. But apparently in both assassinations the men who committed the crimes were far removed from previous direct association with their victims. Perhaps the greatest single factor in causing the murders was the temper of violence in this country in the 1960s. And so, two men, young for their high positions in the affairs of mankind, were deprived of their lives. Families were deprived of two beloved members. The American people and the people on this planet were deprived of two men whose leadership might have affected the very existence of mankind. And these terrible tragedies occurred because of a condition described by Robert Francis Kennedy when he said, "Whenever men take the law into their own hands, the loser is the law—and when the law loses, freedom languishes."